What Do I Want?

What Do I Want?

by Enze Yang (pen name)
Real name on record

Printed in the United States of America

ISBN: 979-8-9944390-2-9 (paperback)

Cover design by Mark K.
Published by Enze Yang Press LLC

First Edition · 2026

A Note on Two Books

On the Road, Also in the World and *What Do I Want?*
stand like the two banks of the same river of life—
echoing one another, yet flowing in opposite directions.

On the Road, Also in the World
opens with lightness and gentleness.
It begins with city lights, street corners, and the warmth
of travel,
moving gradually inward, toward the depths of the soul.
The book comes to rest in its final piece, *Homecoming
of the Soul—*
a closing work that faces the pain of losing a child
and gathers that pain into light.

Homecoming
is the moment when the loss of a child—
what appears, in human terms, as an irrevocable
separation—

is brought to rest in the light of God.

This is the spiritual core of the book:
at the deepest rupture of human life,
light is seen descending inward from eternity.

What Do I Want?, by contrast,
begins with the weight of life itself:
the wilderness, the fractures of systems,
the struggle of the soul, and the silence of God.
It moves steadily toward light, opening along the way—
six seals questioned, guided, guarded, connected,
illuminated, and refined;
the seventh seal waits—breath, stillness, rest.

At last,
the soul slows and grows light
in the embrace of the Lamb.

If *On the Road, Also in the World*
is a journey from the outer world inward,
What Do I Want?
is a passage from the inner life toward the light.

One moves from lightness into weight,
the other from weight into light;
one enters through landscape,
the other ends in breath.

They meet at the same destination:
a human life walking through the world,
and a soul returning home in love.

Dedication 1

Preface · From Fear to Writing 2

General Preface · The Seven Seals 6

What Do I Want? 10

     Journey Map 13

    Chapter 1 · The Question Beyond the Wall 14

    Chapter 2 · Into the Village............................ 19

    Chapter 3 · Twenty Years Outside the Gate of Grace 34

Exodus 44

    Chapter 1 · The Shift of Seats........................ 46

    Chapter 2 · God's Work, Done by Man?................ 53

    Chapter 3 · When Humans Carry the Ark ? 59

    Chapter 4 · The Day of Audit 66

    Chapter 5 | When the Heart Is Audited: From
    Ledgers to the Soul 71

    Chapter 6 · The Stumbling Pilgrim 79

    Chapter 7 · The Shift of Position 88

The Choice of Endurance 95

    Chapter 1 · A Father's Fury........................... 97

Chapter 2 · Jacob, the Limping One......................102

Chapter 3 · The Light of Companionship 107

Chapter 4 · The Unexpected Lifting....................... 112

Chapter 5 · The Battlefield of Grace 117

The Year of Migration: From Desire to Connection ...127

Closing Prayer · Returning to the Vine...................135

Light, Walking Through the Fog 138

Chapter 1 · Beneath the System 140

Chapter 2 · Invisible Thresholds...........................148

Chapter 3 · Storms at the Beginning 154

Chapter 4 · Walking Together..............................164

Chapter 5 · Light in Silence.................................... 175

Overcomers at the Table with the Lord.....................184

Chapter 1 · The Seven Lamps.............................186

Chapter 2 · Reading Revelation 196

Chapter 3 · The Continuance of Preparation..........204

An Invitation to the Reader................................212

The Scroll of My Life, Opened by the Lamb...............213

Chapter 1 · The Knocking of the Soul (Six Seals) 216

Chapter 2 · The Call within Silence......................... 224

Chapter 3 · The Seventh Seal: The Soul That Waits 231

Final Chapter · The Lamb's Embrace 239

Afterword · The Lamb Is Opening the Scroll 241

Acknowledgments 245

Appendix · Poems 248

The Call of Life 249

Chosen by Grace 252

Dedication

To Xiaomei — a friend I have never met

At a turning point in my life,

you opened a door for me.

You left no address, no voice,

yet your name remained in my heart,

becoming the key that led me into a new world.

We never knew each other, never met face to face,

yet through your single act of sponsorship,

I was able to cross the ocean and step into destiny.

This book is a long-delayed letter to you.

May it be a lamp,

shining for others as you once shone for me.

Thank you, Xiaomei.

Your name I will always remember.

Preface · From Fear to Writing

— Written Before the *What Do I Want?* Series

When I was little, I was most afraid of writing compositions.
Whenever the teacher wrote the four characters *"composition
topic"* on the blackboard, my heart would tighten. Others
began to write at once; I stared at the blank page, not
knowing how to begin.

I never believed I could write, nor did I want to.
Everyone in my family wrote better than I did:
my father read classical texts and recited poetry, quoting lines
with effortless ease;
my younger sister was quick and gifted with words—poetry
came naturally to her;

and my daughter—she was writing poems in elementary school, and by high school her thinking had already surpassed mine.

As for me, I hesitated over every word and had no sense of structure.
I grew used to saying, *"I can't."*
So for a long time, I chose silence, hiding myself in the shadow of *"others are better."*

It was not until later, when I came to the Lord,
that I slowly understood those pains I dared not name,
those shames and grievances buried deep in my heart,
were not without purpose.
They were like seeds hidden in the soil—dark and silent—
yet one day, by God's light and grace, they quietly began to grow.

I did not suddenly become a good writer.
I was simply moved by His love and could no longer remain silent.

I wanted to take up the pen to bear witness to His kindness and mercy;
to write down what only I remember,
yet what others are also living through:
the hardships of childhood, a father's reproach, struggles at work,
the laughter found in poverty, repentance after going astray,
and the hand that upheld me through countless low valleys.

I write not because I am confident,
but because I have hope.
I am willing to write even when words fall short, to speak of
God's love;
I am willing to speak even when my voice is small, to testify
to His grace.

The stories of the Bible are not epics written by heroes for
heroes,
but echoes written by the weak for the weak.
Every writer is someone the Lord has raised up from the
words *"I cannot."*

So I began this series, **What Do I Want?**
Not because the answers are clear, but because the longing is
real.
I want to know what I have truly been seeking in this life.
I want to look back and see how, amid struggle and prayer,
God has again and again shown me the way forward.

For me, writing is not the flowering of ability,
but a response to love.

If you, like me, have never believed you could write,
then we are fellow travelers.
May you, as you read these words,
hear the God who does not abandon you say softly:

**"Child, you may begin to speak—
I am listening."**

Some of the institutional experiences described in this book
draw from different workplaces and periods of my
professional life.
For narrative coherence and clarity,
these experiences have been shaped and juxtaposed,
and do not refer to any specific organization or individual.

What these essays seek to explore
is lived experience within systems,
rather than the factual record of particular companies or
events.

General Preface · The Seven Seals

Revelation tells us that the Lamb opened the seven seals—

a great vision concerning history and the future.

What I write here as "seven seals"

are but the marks of my own life.

They cannot be compared with the seven seals of Scripture.

I am but a small drop in the ocean,

offering these fragments as a testimony.

The path of faith is not a straight ascent,

but like a winding river:

sometimes rushing, sometimes stagnant;

sometimes clear, sometimes murky.

In poverty I learned perseverance,

in migration I tasted slumber and return,

in the fog of the workplace I learned to walk with others and to keep watch.

None of this was my own design,

but step by step, God's leading grace.

Placed under the light of the Cross,

my journey reveals a deeper chain of passage:

Seal	Meaning of the Cross	Chapter
First Seal	Calling — from "What I want" to "What He asks of me"	*What Do I Want?*
Second Seal	Beginning — from bondage to freedom	*Exodus*
Third Seal	Obedience — lessons in the wilderness	*The Choice of Perseverance*
Fourth Seal	Return — from wandering to belonging	*The Year of Migration*
Fifth Seal	Community — recognizing one another	*Light, Walking Together in the Fog*

Seal	Meaning of the Cross	Chapter
		in the cracks of the system
Sixth Seal	Refining — healed and invited	*The Overcomer at the Table with the Lord*
Seventh Seal	Witness — the Lamb is opening	*To Bear Witness: The Scroll of My Life*

This book is not a theological commentary,

nor a calculation of the future.

It is a journey of the soul—

between fear and hope,

between failure and grace,

hearing again and again the knock of the Lord.

And so I have come to understand:

Victory is not won by my strength,

but by the identity given through His blood.

He stands at the door and knocks—

not to condemn, not to judge,

but to invite gently:

"I long to dine with you."

May this scroll of mine

become something you and I both hear:

the Lord still knocks, still waits,

until we open the door,

and sit at the table with Him.

Amen

What Do I Want?

General Introduction | The Light That Comes Through a Question

Some questions are not asked to be answered, but to awaken.

"What do you want?"

This question has followed me through the years—

quietly, patiently, sometimes in places where I did not expect it:

at the edges of power in the American workplace,

in the heavy silence of a mountain village in China,

and through the wandering years of a heart looking for home.

Each time, I thought I knew what I wanted.

I said I wanted freedom, dignity, opportunity, achievement.

I reached, I worked, I struggled.

And yet, in my striving, I missed the real desire beneath it all.

This book is both a looking back and a response.

It is not a record of what I have accomplished,

but a story of the moment when I finally understood:

True fulfillment is not found in what I seek,

but in the One who asks me, "What do you want?"

May you, as you read, hear that same question—

not as judgment, not as pressure,

but as invitation.

Like morning light quietly opening the room.

Like a gentle warmth reaching the places we keep hidden.

Like someone calling your name—not loudly, but clearly.

This is a journey traced by that light—

through walls that could not be seen,

into a village where silence shaped destiny,

across a wilderness where the heart resisted surrender—

until, in the echo of that question,

a home was found.

Journey Map

From the unseen walls of the workplace

to the silence of the village.

From the first cry of youth

to the long wandering of the wilderness.

At every step, the same quiet question returns:

"What do you want?"

Chapter 1 · The Question Beyond the Wall

Introduction

Some walls are invisible, yet harder than stone.
Some questions look simple, yet reach the deepest
places of the heart.
On the road toward belonging and fairness, we often
become occupied with survival and forget the first
longing that stirred within us.
But one quiet question has never stopped returning:
"What do you want?"

The day was bright, sunlight warm on my shoulders,
when I walked into ABC Company, a global organization
headquartered in Washington, D.C. I entered with
expectation. Its reputation was excellent; its benefits
were well known. Everything on the surface was orderly,
polished, welcoming.

Yet within the first week, I sensed something beneath
that surface—
an order firm, guarded, and closed.
A place where one could remain, but not without cost.

My work involved managing cash flow, payroll, and
monthly financial reconciliation. Headquarters
supervised more than thirty branches across Asia,
Africa, and Latin America. For many in those branches,
a transfer to D.C. meant hope for a green card—
and the possibility of a different life.

The staff came from many nations and cultures. People
gathered in small, unspoken circles. And although white
employees were not the majority, the decisions,
approval lines, and final power all flowed through them.

It was then I understood something I had never seen so
clearly before:

Numbers do not determine power.
Structure does.
Position does.
Rules do.

On the surface, everyone was courteous, professional.
But beneath that courtesy was a quiet vigilance—
conversations measured, expressions watched, alliances
subtle.
A small oversight could be quickly escalated.
An inquiry from leadership could arrive sooner than a
colleague's smile.
Careful silence often felt safer than honest speech.

In all my years of working, I had never encountered a
place where power was so gentle on the outside—
and so precise underneath.

There was bias here—
not loud, not obvious,
not the kind that makes headlines.
It lived in systems,
in habits,
in what went unsaid.
Not shouted,
but settled.
Such things are harder to name,
and even harder to move.

For freedom and equality, I had come to America
twenty-five years earlier.
I believed I had entered, belonged, arrived.
I lived here, worked here, even reached management.
And still, an invisible wall stood quietly before me—
measuring my skin, my history, my voice.

The distance between being present and being accepted
was wider than I had ever imagined.

I remembered the story in the Gospel of John.
Two disciples followed Jesus.
Jesus turned and asked them,
"What do you want?"
They answered with a request for a place to stay.
But the question itself was deeper than shelter.
It was about longing—
about direction—
about the movement of the heart.

In the workplace, before those unseen walls,
I often answered only the questions of survival:
systems, expectations, performance.
But my soul was being asked another question,
quietly, steadily, without urgency or anger:

"What do you want?"

Prejudice does not disappear overnight.
Walls do not crumble at once.
But the question remained—
gentle, patient, unchanged.

People may think this is a question of adulthood,
of careers, identity, belonging.
But the truth is this:

The shadow of the wall began long before I entered any office.
It began in a place without buildings tall enough to cast shadows—
a mountain village where silence itself shaped destiny.

There, the walls were not built of stone,
but of birth, custom, and fate.
And it was there, on that quiet soil,
that I first learned to call on God.

Chapter 2 · Into the Village

Introduction

Some places are not marked on any map, yet lie hidden deep in a person's destiny.

Some systems are not written on paper, yet are carved into every life.

When I asked, *"What do I want?"* the answer was not only freedom and dignity,

but also a space where truth could be spoken,

a world where no one need bow the head.

To step into the village was not merely to enter barren soil,

but to walk into a silence of destiny—

so heavy that even starlight dared not fall on it.

And still I kept asking: *"What do I want?"*

During the Cultural Revolution, our home was ransacked, my father arrested.

At school I became an outcast, always the subject of whispers and pointing fingers.

At that time, my greatest wish was simply to lift my head, to breathe freely, and not be despised.

I was born in China, raised in that era.

There, discrimination and injustice were not drawn along the color of skin,

yet they cut just as deeply into the bone.

Birth could determine fate; silence was the only means of survival.

In 1970, my parents were sent down to the mountains of Hubei Province,

and naturally, my younger sister and I followed.

At dusk, a truck carried us and all our belongings to the commune.

The peasants who came to receive us were already waiting.

There was no road from the commune to the production team—only footsteps and torchlight.

They hoisted our belongings with ropes, balanced them on their shoulders, and lit torches.

We trailed behind, walking through the night toward a place destined to mark our lives forever.

Some roads can only be finished in the dark;

some places are carved only into the heart.

That night we walked not only into a mountain village, but into the depths of destiny itself.

The commune had only one junior high school. It was a humble place, with just two classes, offering only two subjects: mathematics and Chinese.

During the first week, we had a composition class.

The teacher said: *"Write an essay about the Mid-Autumn Festival."*

Almost every student began the same way:

"At this time of national celebration, we must remember that our fellow countrymen in Taiwan are still living in the depths of misery..."

They wrote fluently, for these words had long been memorized by heart.

Suddenly, the teacher stopped and read out another essay:

"The full moon hangs in the sky.

A breeze slips through the osmanthus tree behind the house, carrying a touch of coolness.

Today is the Mid-Autumn Festival.

No one mentions it, and no one celebrates it.

Only, looking out the window, tonight's moon seems especially round.

A bucket in front of the door holds another moon, smaller, yet quietly glowing.

Everyone at home has fallen asleep except me.

I think of my elder sister. Wherever she may be, perhaps at this very moment she too is looking up at the moon.

I seem to see her standing alone in its light. Perhaps she is thinking of home. Perhaps she is thinking of me.

We are in different places, yet we gaze at the same moon, sharing the same moment.

Through the moon, I seem to see her face; and I know, she can also see mine.

Today is a quiet Wednesday. Only my heart feels a little more joyful."

The classroom fell silent. No one laughed. No one moved.

The teacher set down the paper and said, *"This is the most sincere essay."*

At home I hurried to tell my mother, excited that the teacher had read my essay and praised me.

But my mother did not smile. She quietly closed the door and said:

"Don't write like that again."

"Why?"

"Because you wrote too sincerely. You said your sister was standing alone—that will make people say you are dissatisfied with life.

To be dissatisfied with life is to be dissatisfied with the government."

She lowered her voice:

"You thought it was an essay. Others will treat it as testimony.

You thought it was the voice of your heart. Others will take it as confession."

In that moment I understood: words are not just words.

They can be evidence of iron, or they can be shackles.

That winter, I traded my pen for slogans and locked my thoughts inside my head.

It was the first time I realized—there are places that even the moon and sun dare not light.

In the classroom, to speak truth was dangerous.

In the village, especially for girls, destiny was already ruled by custom—

not by what you liked, not by what you chose.

On winter nights, girls sat together, threading needles through cloth,

stitch by stitch making shoes for their future husbands and in-laws.

This was part of the marriage contract.

Whether they liked it or not, the shoes would eventually be placed beneath a man's feet.

Most girls were betrothed at fourteen.

"Have you met him?" I asked.

"Once."

"Have you spoken?"

"No."

"Then how do you know what kind of person he is?"

"It doesn't matter. Liking him is luck. Not liking him is fate."

They spoke calmly, as if discussing the weather.

Lanlan was my friend, sixteen, her smile showing a row of even teeth.

Next year she would be married. One day she came to me, her face dark and heavy.

That day was her brother's wedding.

"Why aren't you at home helping?"

"Weddings are not women's business."

"Why not?"

She fell silent. *"That is men's business."*

Only then did I learn of a custom in these weddings—

Before the banquet, the men would shove the groom out of the bridal chamber and slam the bride down onto its floor, and swarm over her, tearing at her pants.

From sixty-year-old elders down to sixteen-year-old boys,

whoever loosened the belt first could carry her to the bridal bed and do as he pleased.

To protect themselves, brides wore multiple layers of pants, tying the knots as tightly as they could.

If tied well, they could not be undone for an entire day.

They called it *"festivity,"* a way to bring *"good luck"* to the groom's family.

On the wedding night, men piled onto the bride like players in an American football tackle.

No one thought it was wrong.

No one spoke the word *"dignity"*—perhaps because it had never been taught.

That moment, my chest tightened until I could not breathe.

What kind of custom was this?

It was naked trampling, brutal violation of women.

We knew too well the sorrow of being female, yet we could not break free.

It was not festivity but collective assault;

not tradition but institutionalized silence.

From then on, I studied even harder—

not only for myself, but for the girls who would never have the chance to read.

I wanted to study, because only knowledge could carry me out of this land of silence.

Yet my fate had been nailed to the bottom rung of society from birth.

Our family belonged to the *Five Black Categories*—

landlords, rich peasants, counterrevolutionaries, bad elements, rightists.

My father was a rightist, my grandfather a counterrevolutionary, my maternal grandfather a great landlord and an educator.

With such a background, entering high school was almost impossible.

At that time, I had never read the Bible, nor heard anyone speak the name of God.

But when people cannot save themselves, the heart instinctively turns toward an unseen place.

Fate was like a wall; I crashed against it again and again, never breaking through.

Until one night, I decided to be silent no more.

I did not know God's name. I did not know how to pray.

But I knew this: if I did not cry out, I would remain trapped behind that wall forever.

That night, the kerosene lamp flickered.

I quietly closed the door.

I had no lofty words, only clumsy sentences to voice my longing:

"Most High God in heaven, I want to study—

I want to enter high school and continue   my education.

I want to leave this place.

But I was born among the Five Black Categories.

Without Your protection, I cannot continue in school.

Have mercy on me."

And a miracle happened.

In that village where even the moon dared not shine, He heard my first cry.

I received my high school admission letter.

That day our whole family rejoiced as if it were New Year.

Mother said she had heard magpies calling loudly on the branches that morning—

she never thought such good news would really come to our home.

The new high school was far from home, and I had to board there.
The dormitory was free, but the cafeteria served only teachers.
Every student had to carry a load of firewood each month to the school, to steam the rice and cook the vegetables.

On the day school started, I carried firewood and bedding on my shoulders and walked up the winding mountain road.
The thought of finally being able to study filled me with joy, and I did not feel tired.
It was as if wings were on my feet—
the ten miles of mountain road passed in a blink.

The school stood on a hillside, a few low houses shaped like the Chinese character "﹂."
In the middle was the playground, with classrooms and dormitories on both sides.
There were only six girls in the entire school, all living in

the same dormitory.
Three bunk beds lined the wall; I slept on the top.

The mountains were poor.
The windows had no glass, only sheets of white plastic
film.
The school had no electricity, no running water, no
coal—
and I had never even heard the word "gas."

We ate only two meals a day, one at eleven in the
morning, one at five in the afternoon.
At dawn we rose, washed, measured rice into bowls,
added water, and sent them to the kitchen steamer.
After class we would collect our bowls and eat in the
classroom.

There was little food to bring from home.
Mother gave me a jar of fermented bean curd.
That jar became my only side dish, day after day, meal
after meal—
until I could not bear to look at it.
In the end, I ate plain rice—alone.

During evening study, eight students sat around a
kerosene lamp in the corner.
The faint light flickered across their thin faces.
Each was bent over his work, absorbed, as if the whole
world were nothing but that lamp and those pages.
Who would have thought that years later, several of
these students would enter college?

The village children were poorer than we were.
Most could not afford toothpaste and hardly brushed
their teeth;
some had no rice at all, surviving only on steamed dried
sweet potatoes.
For them, to sit in a classroom was already a rare
privilege.
Many had never been to the county town, never seen a
train,
could not imagine how an airplane rose into the sky.

Their hunger for knowledge, their concentration in
reading, commanded respect.
I truly hoped that one day, we could all walk out of these
mountains and see the world beyond.

At night, to relieve ourselves, we had to cross the
playground swallowed by darkness.
When there was no moon, we struck a match—
borrowing its brief, trembling spark to see the pit
latrine,
before placing our feet down with care.
In those years, a flashlight was a luxury;
the only light we could afford
was the flare of a match.

There were few books to read.
One classmate had a battered, incomplete volume of
Tang poetry, which I borrowed.

When I read Du Fu's *"Happy Rain on a Spring Night,"*
my heart leapt with joy:

Good rain knows its season; it comes when spring arrives.
Stealthily, it enters the night, nurturing all things in silence.
Dark clouds cover the country paths; on the river, a single light shines.
At dawn, the red, wet earth reveals flowers heavy with bloom in Chengdu.

The mountains were beautiful; the water sweet.
In the morning, mist curled among the peaks, and the pines stood silent in stillness.
Yet wrong policies left fertile soil unable to sustain life.

The years of hardship tempered the will of youth,
engraving deep marks into our lives.
In those days, we sought knowledge on barren ground,
lit matches in the darkness,
and fought for a space of light against fate.

Cultural fracture and material scarcity pushed people to the margins.
But even in the poorest villages, the thirst for knowledge remained—
clear as spring water, stubborn as morning mist.

Poverty taught us endurance.
But more importantly, it taught us not to be defined by it.

Knowledge could not immediately change reality,
but it gave us the power to understand the world,
and the possibility of choice.

I did not know then
that this hunger for learning would one day carry me
out of the mountains
and lead me into a wider wilderness.
I did not know then that the hunger for knowledge was
also a hunger for grace.

There, I would once more hear that question:
"What do you want?"
This time, it was no longer a whisper in the night,
but a voice that pressed upon the whole of my life.

Chapter 3 · Twenty Years Outside the Gate of Grace

Introduction: From "What Do I Want" to "What He Asks Me"

A human life is often spent chasing the question, *"What do I want?"*

We think we desire opportunities, achievements, dignity—even the right to escape suffering.

Yet along the way, God keeps asking us: *"What do you want?"*

It is not that He does not hear our prayers,

but that He waits for us to awaken from chasing after "food that perishes,"

and to turn toward the "food that endures to eternal life."

I once ran hard to escape poverty and discrimination,

longing to stand in the sunlight without lowering my head.

But on that road, again and again I missed His call.

It was a wilderness journey—

not because God was unwilling to lead me into the promised land,

but because I was unwilling to lay down my own stubbornness.

That hunger for knowledge had once carried me out of the mountains.

After the fall of Lin Biao, the "sent-down" cadres returned to the cities.

Since I was still in school, I returned with my parents to Wuhan and was able to finish high school.

In 1976, the Cultural Revolution ended.

China began to change dramatically.

In 1977, the college entrance exam was restored.

The moment I held my admission ticket in hand, I was overcome with joy.

I had never imagined I would one day qualify to sit for the exam.

At that time, I also prayed to God, asking Him to keep me.

But I had never set my heart to know Him, to experience Him, or to consider who He truly was.

My prayers were cries for help, not a relationship, not a connection with Him.

I passed the exam, entered university, and after graduation stayed on to teach.

The tide of reform and opening pushed open another door.

In 1988, I left for America to pursue graduate studies at Ohio University.

On campus, there was a Chinese Bible study group, mostly students from Taiwan.

I was warmly invited to join, and I agreed.

That was my first time truly reading the Bible.

It was a summer night.

The air outside was hot, filled with the ceaseless sound of cicadas.

Inside, the air conditioner blew cool air, bringing a pleasant relief.

They took turns reading Scripture, voices clear and focused.

Some eyes shone bright, as if they truly saw a path before them.

Some took notes; others nodded in response.

But I was distracted.

That night, we read John 6:

"Do not labor for the food that perishes, but for the food that endures to eternal life, which the Son of Man will give you."

What a good word, what a gospel of life!

Yet I could not take in a single sentence.

I thought to myself, *"This book is written for the rich."*

The rich, who never worry about hunger, of course seek eternal life.

I, who could hardly fill my stomach—how could I think of eternity?

From that day on, I never returned to the Bible study.

In that remote mountain village, I had once cried out to God for the chance to study.

He heard me, and He granted it.

But when I entered university, when I stepped into a wider world,

I did not carry gratitude into knowing Him.

At Ohio University, I had the chance to read the Bible.

I was surrounded by so many devout Christians, a cloud of witnesses.

Yet I refused to open myself,

refused to learn God's word alongside them.

Every day I hurried out early and came home late,

thinking only of graduating quickly, finding a job, earning money.

Everything else I regarded as distraction.

Looking back now, I see—

sin in me was simply laid bare.

Not as malice against God,

but as hiding spiritual poverty beneath the cloak of "realistic anxiety."

Not as denial of His existence,

but as being consumed by worry over "food that perishes,"

too bound to look up and see the "food that endures to eternal life."

Sin is not always hostility.

It can be indifference.

It can be neglect.

It can be silence at the very gate of grace.

It is like a thin, invisible film covering the heart,

so that even while standing in the light, one does not lift the head.

Grace stretched out its hand again and again,

and my soul missed it again and again.

That summer night,

the air conditioner cooled the room,

but my heart was parched like a desert.

I sat in the corner of the Bible study, the door of my heart shut tight.

From my first cry to God until I truly received Him,

twenty years passed.

Those twenty years were like Israel's wandering in the wilderness—

not because God was unwilling to bring me into the promised land,

but because I would not lay down my stubborn will.

In that long stretch of time,

I tasted both spiritual and earthly pain.

It was not revenge,

but another form of grace—

not soft or sentimental,

but framed by justice and pulsing with mercy.

It shaped me. It called me.

God never abandoned me.

Even when I shut the door, He stood outside waiting.

Even when I went my own way, His hand still rested on my shoulder.

I came to know Him, not because I was wiser,

but because He never ceased to reveal Himself to me.

What do I want?

I once thought I wanted a way forward—

an admission letter,

a visa,

a respectable job,

a stable income.

I longed to escape discrimination,

to break free from poverty,

to stand in the sunlight without lowering my head,

without shame,

without being shoved by fate.

For these goals I ran with all my strength,

praying for God's help—

yet never considering that what He longed to give me

was far beyond what I could ask or imagine.

He asked me, *"What do you want?"*

And I only pointed to the suffering before me, saying,
"Let me pass."

But He waited for me to lift my eyes

and see what truly gives freedom and satisfaction—

not opportunities, not achievements,

but fellowship with Him, Himself.

In my first cries, I treated God as a storeroom,

asking only that He keep supplying what I lacked.

But after I walked through the wilderness, tasting its sweetness and bitterness,

I slowly came to understand:

True hunger is not in the stomach, but in the soul.

True belonging is not in nations or classes, but in His embrace.

Today, when the Lord again asks me, *"What do you want?"*

I no longer evade.

Lord, I want You—

to know You, to draw near to You, to dwell in You,

as a branch abides in the vine.

I want You to live in me,

so that all I do and think is pleasing in Your sight.

I want Your own life to fill me,

no longer measuring my worth by the world's standards.

What do I want?

—I want You. You alone.

Apart from this, I have no other desire.

Exodus

General Preface

There was no wilderness—only a conference room.

No Red Sea—only ledgers and account sheets.

No golden calf—yet somewhere between feng shui and bank loans,

we were still drawing the boundary of who holds sovereignty.

Exodus here is not a journey of geography,

but a turning of faith.

A believer who works with numbers sits among spreadsheets—

and also sits behind Moses—

asking a question that has never grown old:

Can the work of God be carried by human hands?

Can faith breathe inside a budget table?

And in our most devout attempts to "help,"

are we quietly steadying the Ark of the Covenant?

So this is not merely a story of "changing seats."

It is a journey of wrestling for the right place of faith

between numbers and reality.

This story is written for all who stand between
sovereignty and circumstance—

between emails and prayers,

growth targets and obedience.

May you find in these pages

a reason to depart,

and a posture with which to return.

Chapter 1 · The Shift of Seats

Introduction

A seat may change—
but sovereignty does not.

A person can move a chair to the southeast to ward off misfortune,
yet God calls the heart to turn toward Him for true light.

The adjustments of feng shui are light as dust;
the turning of faith is weighty as destiny.

The world concerns itself with where to place the chair.
Believers, instead, listen for the voice that asks:
Who is inviting me to sit?

The wisdom of this age often trades calling for comfort,
and disguises convenience as obedience.

Perhaps the spiritual journey begins right here—
in one reluctant, unexpected shift of a seat.

At 7:45 a.m., I pushed open the glass door of the office,
just as I always did.
The air still held the faint warmth of last night's coffee.
Boxes rustled and thudded as people packed and moved
things around.

My coworkers were already busy at their desks, and I
walked toward the window-side desk that had been
mine for three years, stepping through the soft coolness
of the morning light.

Our Chief Financial Officer leaned out from the break
room, wearing the same polite smile as always.
"Today we're switching the accounting team with Sales,"
he said. "We'll be trading offices."

I paused, my eyes instinctively returning to my old
seat—
where every morning, sunlight fell across my keyboard,
and the steam from my coffee drifted upward through
the light.

It was close to the door, easy to reach, and from there I
could watch the constant flow of cars outside and the
changing sky throughout the day.

As I passed Wendy's desk—the accounts receivable clerk—I asked in a low voice,
"Do you know why we're suddenly changing seats?"

She was sorting papers into a box and answered half-jokingly,
"Sales numbers have been down. I heard the boss brought in a feng shui master.
The master said we accountants sitting by the window 'let the money leak out.'
If Sales sits by the windows, the energy rises—and business comes in."

I couldn't help but laugh.
Wasn't our boss a devout Christian?
If God is the One who provides,
how could the placement of chairs determine profit or loss?

As I packed my belongings, I whispered to myself a verse I had long known by heart:
"My God will meet all your needs according to the riches of His glory in Christ Jesus."

And suddenly, the scene of the Israelites in the wilderness rose before my mind:
how they had seen God part the Red Sea, rain manna from heaven—
yet still cast a golden calf to worship.

Moses was faithful, yet his generation—except for Joshua and Caleb—never entered the Promised Land.

Then I thought of myself when I first joined the company three years earlier.
Back then, the boss was in his prime—handsome, composed, his voice deep and warm.
He was a sincere believer, gentle in manner, and his home radiated peace.

His wife cooked beautifully and played the piano with grace.
Every Friday evening, they hosted Bible study gatherings—
the house full of the fragrance of dinner and the quiet sound of hymns.
There was a deep sense of rest there.

My coworkers often invited me to join.
At first, I declined—I was tired, or busy, or simply unsure.
But eventually, I decided to go once,
just to see what this book called the Bible was really about.

That evening happened to be the start of Genesis, chapter one.
Everyone read slowly, sentence by sentence, noticing every detail.

I listened at first with a skeptical sort of curiosity.
Was the Bible truly profound—
or simply ancient mythology made sacred by repetition?

But as time passed, I found myself drawn to the stories of Abraham, Isaac, and Jacob.

I wanted to understand why Abraham was called the father of faith.

What moved me most was not his heroism, but his change.
He left Ur of the Chaldeans because God called him—
and on that journey he knew hunger, conflict, fear.

He even lied to protect his life, saying Sarah was his sister.
Pharaoh favored him because of her beauty—until God intervened.

The Bible did not portray him as perfect.
He was afraid.
He stumbled.
He lied.
And yet—
God still called him.
And still used him.

I had always assumed faith was for idealists—
for the strong, the extraordinary.
But in Abraham, I saw someone very ordinary—
someone who simply stepped out of his comfort.

When he later rescued Lot with 318 household men,
and when he refused the wealth of the king of Sodom—
"For I have sworn to the Lord, God Most High... that I
will accept nothing, not even a thread or a sandal
strap..."—
I felt something in me tremble.

Faith was not a concept.
It was a recognition of the Source.

I bowed my head.
I knew then that I needed God's salvation.
Not because I was worthy—
but because I was weak.

That night, I accepted Christ and became a believer.

But now, three years later—
though the memory of that grace still lived in me—
reality pressed close and uneasy.

Could a believer truly find alignment
between faith and the world we walk in?

This seat change seemed like a small matter—
yet it asked a very old question:

Faith is not merely something spoken.
It is a matter of sovereignty.

If Jesus is Lord,
then His kingdom must reign in my heart—

not in theory,
but in the smallest of decisions,
even in the rearrangement of desks.

Chapter 2 · God's Work, Done by Man?

Introduction

The footsteps of faith fall upon the floors of everyday
life.
We long to do God's work, yet rarely discern
when we have crossed into what belongs to Him alone.

Between prayer and decision
there lies a line that cannot be seen—
where human devotion becomes tangled
with the sovereignty of God.

It is not that we refuse obedience;
it is that we do not always know

when to move
and when to be still.

After the Bible study ended, I stayed behind to help tidy
the kitchen.
Most people had already left.
Only the boss remained in the living room, leaning back
on the sofa, a cup of tea warming his hands.

He looked tired.

I was about to say goodbye when he spoke.
"Do you have a moment? Sit with me. I want to talk."

I hesitated, then nodded and took a seat across from
him.

He was quiet for a long moment before saying,
"You must think I'm... not very spiritual."

His tone held no defensiveness—only honesty.
I didn't know how to respond.

He looked toward the dark window.
"The feng shui thing—you must have found it hard to
understand."

I answered softly, "It did surprise me."

He gave a faint, weary laugh.
"The consultant I invited has an unusual background.
Studied environmental science in China, then
researched spatial flow and magnetic field theory in
Hong Kong.
He claims feng shui is a complex system—what Western
scholars call environmental psychology.

You know I studied engineering.
Layout and structure… they've always made sense to
me."

I said nothing. I simply listened.

He continued:
"To be honest, I struggled with it.
Of course I know God is the source of provision, the
Lord of all things.
But business is hard.
Competition grows, prices fall, and if a client doesn't
reply for a day, you can lose millions.
You know how many families this company supports."

I nodded.

He looked at me with a weary sincerity.
"I've always thought—if God has given me this company
to run, then I have to do everything I can to keep it
going.

Moses had to fight battles.
Joshua still had to cross the river, lead armies, march

around Jericho.
When God chooses people, doesn't He ask them to
complete His work?
Aren't we, in a sense, tools in His hands?"

His eyes were not defensive.
They were earnest.
And tired.
He truly believed what he was saying.

He went on quietly:
"Sometimes I feel the company has survived because
I've held this place for God.
We host Bible study. We give. We pray.
Isn't this honoring Him?
I know I fall short. But at least here—there is still
Scripture. Still prayer."

There was conviction in his voice—almost a vow he had
made to himself.

I was silent for a while.
Then a scene from Scripture rose sharply in my mind.

When David brought the Ark of the Covenant back to
Jerusalem,
the oxen stumbled, and Uzzah reached out to steady the
Ark.
He wasn't wicked.
He acted out of reverence, instinct, alarm—

and yet he was struck down.
All Israel trembled.

I spoke softly:
"Yes, God does use people—Moses, Joshua, Isaiah.
They carried great responsibility.
But because of that, God required a holiness even greater."

He listened without interrupting.

"Sometimes we truly do want to help God make things work," I said.
"But God is not only concerned with outcomes.
Uzzah may have meant well—but God was not pleased.
Because God does not need us to steady His work.
He asks for obedience."

His eyes shifted—something inside him stirred.
Then, very quietly, he asked:
"Do you think... I am like Uzzah?"

I answered gently,
"I cannot judge that.
But I think you are very tired.
You carry the weight of the business, the ministry, the giving, the people.
But have you asked God which part is truly yours to carry—
and which part is His alone?"

He lowered his head and said nothing.

The room was very still.
Outside, the trees swayed softly in the streetlight.

I remained silent too—because I sensed that God was
already speaking to him.

When I finally stood to leave, he walked me to the door.
"Thank you," he said quietly. "What you said tonight... I
will think about it."

I looked into his tired yet sincere eyes,
and a thought rose in me:

We all stand at the edge of the wilderness,
longing for the promised land.

And perhaps the greatest temptation
is not worshiping the golden calf—
but believing we can steady the Ark
with our own hands.

Chapter 3 · When Humans Carry the Ark ?

Introduction

The work of God often appears to require human hands—
yet it cannot be carried out by human methods alone.

We lift tools, fix our eyes on outcomes,
and forget this simple truth:
If the Ark is not raised according to God's command,
even the hand that reaches out to steady it
may provoke Him.

In the house of God, action is not bravado—
it is the discipline of obedience.

When we walk ahead of Him,
even our most devout labor
can become the hand of Uzzah.

In just a few short years, the company had grown from
an obscure startup
into a rising name in the industry.
The boss expanded distribution channels, sent teams
across the country,
opened regional branches from north to south.

Sales took off like a helicopter lifting vertically into the
sky—
from one million a month
to ten million—
a climb so rapid
people could not help but stare.

It was expansion—
ambitious, dazzling,
but far from steady.

We were wholesalers of computer components imported
from Taiwan.
Shipments left the port of Kaohsiung, crossed the
Pacific to Los Angeles,
and from there our team scattered them to retailers
across the United States.

Most transactions were bulk orders.
Customers rarely paid immediately—
fifteen days was fast; thirty was normal.
Meanwhile, our Taiwanese suppliers demanded
payment upon delivery,
without delay.

And so cash became a restless river—
the goods had already gone out,
but the money had not yet returned.
The company lived at the water's edge,
trying not to slip.

The boss decided to speak with the bank.
He brought me and the finance director, Lin,
to meet a loan officer named Mike—
a middle-aged white man with sharp eyes,
a crisp suit, and sentences trimmed of all excess.

"Mr. Zhang," he said, flipping through the statements,
brow tightening,
"we've noticed your accounts receivable have been
stretching
over the past three months."

The boss smiled calmly.
"Yes. To maintain long-term partnerships,
we've extended payment terms for some of our older
clients."

Mike nodded, but the firmness in his tone did not
soften.

"Even so, the proportion past ninety days exceeds our
risk threshold.
Our lending ratios are fixed—
thirty-day receivables are financed at ninety percent,
sixty-day at seventy,
ninety-day at forty.
Beyond that, we no longer lend."

Lin spoke gently,
"Year-end closing caused delays across the board.
We're actively collecting—payments should clear soon."

Mike met her eyes.
"We understand business cycles.
But risk policies are non-negotiable.
Our credit decisions follow performance,
not intention."

I sat listening, noting every word.

The boss paused, then smiled again.
"Don't worry, Mike.
We'll bring the sales numbers back up."

"I do believe in your capability," Mike replied,
closing the folder with clinical precision.
"But the bank responds to data, not confidence.
Please ensure next quarter's statements meet target,
or we will tighten your credit line."

When he left, the room fell into a heavy quiet.
Lin looked down at the reports and murmured,
"He left faster this time."

I turned toward the window.
Sunlight flooded the glass—
but it could not warm
the faint chill rising inside me.

"What now?" I asked.

She exhaled softly.
"The boss says to wait.
He'll find a way to raise the sales figures."

"How?"

She didn't answer.
She simply closed the binder—
as if shutting a door
none of us wished to open.

A few days later,
the sales numbers did rise.

Several new "large orders" appeared.
The accounts receivable column filled again—
neatly, conveniently, reassuringly.

The bank released the funds.
Payroll went out.

Operations continued—
smooth, orderly, almost serene.

But I knew:
Growth was becoming something that needed to
appear—
whether or not it was real.

Spring arrived.
Flowers burst open outside—bright, abundant, fearless.

Inside the office,
phones rang nonstop,
keyboards rattled like rain on metal.

The cash flow ran at high pressure,
every link pulled tight.
No one dared slow down.
No one dared admit exhaustion.

The boss grew quieter.
Lin held the system together out of habit more than
hope.

The azaleas outside were blooming in fierce color;
the atmosphere inside was wound like wire.

I sat typing in my corner,
but inside a question was forming—

a small one at first,
then sharper, heavier, truer:

Perhaps the real crisis was not declining sales.
Perhaps the deeper crisis
was that we had gone too long without asking:

Was this truly the work of God?

Or were we, in our earnestness,
merely trying—
with the best of intentions—
to carry out God's work for Him?

Chapter 4 · The Day of Audit

Introduction

Numbers are honest mirrors—
and silent witnesses.

Every entry records a choice;
every invoice carries an intention.

When we sign our name on a document,
are we also leaving an imprint
on our faith?

The one being audited is never only the company—
but the heart we bring
before God.

A few days later, the bank auditors arrived exactly on
schedule.
I had prepared the reports in advance, arranging them
in careful rows across their table.

The audit proceeded with its usual rigor:
every account receivable had to correspond
to a shipping record.

But soon, several large transactions drew attention—
the amounts were clearly recorded,
yet no shipping slips supported them.

A knot tightened in my chest.

I went to the warehouse to find the shipping manager.
He sifted through his logs, page by page, then shook his
head.

"I didn't handle these," he said.

Unease rose in me like a quiet tide.
I pressed it down and went to speak with the boss.

He appeared calm.
"I handled those clients personally," he said.
"The shipping documents are with me."

The next day, he brought in a full stack of slips.
The auditors reviewed them, found everything "in
order,"
and left satisfied.

The audit passed without issue.

But the real problem did not end with the audit.
It only began to surface
in the weeks that followed.

Three months passed.
The payments from those large transactions
never arrived.

Meanwhile, the recorded shipments increased—
larger amounts, more frequent entries—
yet incoming payments remained sparse.

The cash flow began to tighten
like a belt pulled one notch too far.

I went to speak with the finance director.

She answered lightly, almost casually:
"The boss says every business has tight periods.
Friends help each other through.
We just need a long-term view."

It sounded reasonable—
but reason alone could not silence the question forming
inside me:

**Can financial risk truly be carried by
'friendship'?**

We were sustaining operations through loans.
If sales slipped, if interest rates changed,
if even one link in the chain snapped—
what did we have to fall back on?

One afternoon during lunch break,
I ran into the boss's brother-in-law in the break room.

He was drinking coffee, chatting cheerfully
about the new house he had just moved into.

When I heard the address,
I froze.

It was the same address
listed on those large "customer" shipments.

I asked, as casually as I could,
"Are you in sales too?"

He waved his hand and laughed.
"No, not at all.
I don't know anything about that."

A coldness shot through my veins.

The "customers" behind those shipments
might have never existed.

That evening, I walked out of the office alone.
The late autumn wind carried a thin, quiet chill.

The city was full of noise—
cars rushing, people talking—
yet my heart felt still,
heavy as water in a stone basin.

I stood at the edge of the sidewalk,
watching the flow of traffic,
feeling as if every direction had closed.

Faith—
could it speak into something this tangled,
this shadowed,
this painfully real?

These invoices,
these addresses,
these tidy explanations with long shadows behind
them—

they gathered inside me like dark clouds.

I did not know the answer.

But I knew one thing:

I had to begin an audit—
not of the books,
but of my own soul.

Chapter 5 | When the Heart Is Audited: From Ledgers to the Soul

Introduction

The truest audit is not done in the warehouse,
nor in the bank—
but in the quiet hours of the night.

When hymns and spreadsheets sit side by side,
we find ourselves standing at the threshold
between the sacred
and the ordinary.

The weight of faith is not measured
by how devoutly we sing,
but by whether—
in the dust and the pressure—
we still choose
to walk in the light.

It was a Friday evening in late autumn, the air turning
cool.
As usual, I went to the boss's house for Bible study.

The moment the door opened, the familiar smell of
dinner greeted me.
Warm light filled the rooms, and the piano played softly.
Everything looked the same—
yet my heart was heavy.

That night we read Romans chapter six:
dead to sin, alive to God.

Before the study, we sang hymns—gentle, sincere.
I sang too, but the words did not settle into my heart.
My eyes drifted across familiar faces,
and they all felt strangely distant.

God's Word had once been my lamp and my path—
the light that carried me out of the shadows of
childhood,
through political upheaval,
into the freedom of another land.

But now, I wavered.

Could faith truly hold together with reality?

Was the person who sat in the office
the same one who prayed in this living room?

Or had reverence become something we practiced only
on Friday nights,

while our hands carried the dust of the world
for the rest of the week?

The finance director was there too—tall, quiet,
composed.
She sang softly, her expression peaceful, as if nothing
was amiss.
I watched her and wondered:
Had she seen the accounts I saw?
Did her heart tremble as mine did?

The boss led the study.
He read aloud,
"Shall we continue in sin so that grace may abound?
By no means!"

His voice was earnest, familiar—
the same voice I had once trusted without question.

But in my mind the shipping slips returned:
the empty addresses,
the numbers without substance beneath them.

When he explained the passage,
did he think of the company?
Had he wrestled?
Had he resisted?
Or had he silenced his own heart?

I lowered my gaze.

He had been my guide when I first came to faith.
He opened his home.
He gave generously.
He lived visibly as a believer.

And I—
I had come through political chaos, rural hardship,
immigration struggle—
simply trying to survive, to give my daughter a future.
I had not taught, nor preached.
I worked.
I believed quietly.
I respected him.

He was the one who "lived out" his faith.
I was the one who took refuge in it.

But now, with faith and reality colliding,
the question rose:
Had he truly lived out his faith—
or had he learned to keep faith
safely contained within Friday nights?

After the study, I went home but could not sleep.
The night pressed heavily.
The invoices with no receipts,
the explanations that never quite explained—
they weighed on me like stones.

I tried to pray,
but the words felt thin.

So I opened Scripture,
and my Bible fell to Genesis chapter fifteen.

Abraham's vision.
The animals divided.
The dreadful darkness.
And God—alone—passing through the pieces
as smoking fire
and blazing torch.

My breath caught.

It was not a bargain.
Not "You keep your part, and I will keep mine."
It was God binding Himself to His promise
even when man would fail.

In the darkness,
He walked alone.
He would bear it.
He would remain faithful.

I closed my eyes and prayed:
"Lord, I am in the dark.
Walk into it Yourself.
Grant me wisdom.

Grant me courage.
Show me where to step."

From that night on, I examined the accounts again.
Some payments came in—
but the warehouse had no record of shipments.
Still, the transactions were approved.

The more I followed the numbers,
the more the pattern emerged.
The accounts the boss "handled personally"
were tangled, unclear.

The stone in my heart grew heavier.

Philippians 4:6–7 rose in my mind:
"Do not be anxious about anything...
And the peace of God...
will guard your hearts and your minds in Christ Jesus."

So I prayed.
For the company.
And for myself.
Not only for wisdom—
but for courage.

Because the question was no longer about numbers.
It was about how I would respond.

I could remain silent.
If I did not look too closely, did not ask, did not speak,
my job would be safe.

But if I chose silence—
would that not make me a participant?

Could I still say I walked in the light?
Could I still say I believed God?

I looked at the pile of documents before me.
It felt as though every line of numbers was asking:

Will you stand?
Will you remain awake?
Will you choose the light—
even here?

The night was deep.
The city quiet.
Streetlights cast shifting shadows on the floor.

I walked to the window.
The wind stirred the leaves gently—
as though God whispered in the darkness:

"You cannot see everything.
But I am here."

I did not know whether the path ahead
would be wilderness or storm.

I only knew this:
If I was to walk in the light,
I would have to face the dark first—

even if I could take
only
one
step.

Chapter 6 · The Stumbling Pilgrim

Introduction

There are two kinds of journeys in this world:
one is the travel of the body,
and the other is the departure of the soul.

The first crosses mountains and seas;
the second moves through memory and fear.

Some people spend their whole lives searching for
belonging,
yet never pause long enough
to hear the call within.

And sometimes, the true home we seek
is hidden in the very place
we least want to look back on.

That night, I sat by the window in silence.
The streetlight cast a dim glow on the moving shadows
of the trees outside,
and it felt as though memories themselves were stirring.

My daughter had already fallen asleep,
but I stayed awake—not because of deadlines,
but because a question had begun rising quietly within
me:

**Had all my years of striving—crossing oceans,
enduring hardship, fighting for stability—been
only for a job title and a monthly income?**

Faith had taught me to walk in integrity.
Yet I realized I still could not bear to look back at parts
of my past.
When I closed my eyes, memories surged forward like a
tide.

I saw again the day our home was raided during the
Cultural Revolution—
the fear on my mother's face,
the confusion in my own young heart.

Then came the years in the countryside:
poverty, silence, humiliation,
the suffocating sense of being trapped.
Those experiences were not distant;
they lived inside me still.

I had left China, crossed borders,
worked my way forward step by step,
believing that if I worked hard enough,
I could reach a place where I belonged.

But now, facing the unraveling at work,
I found myself asking:

Is this what I crossed the world for?

Hard work had once seemed enough to carve out hope,
but hope had grown hazy,
and the light of faith—once bright—
felt dimmed under the weight of reality.

I grew up in the Cultural Revolution.
I was ten when the Red Guards filled the streets.
Whenever drums thundered in the distance,
my mother would whisper,
"Look—are they coming for us?"
I would peer through the window and answer,
"Not today. They went to the house next door."

But the day still came.
They arrived shouting,
forced us outside,
tore through our home,
burned my father's books in the courtyard.

The fire lit my mother's face.
That image has never left me.

Even now, I cannot bear the sound of heavy drums.
Loud, rhythmic music unsettles me instantly.
Trauma often hides quietly in the body;
some wounds do not fade simply because time has
passed.

Before we left for the countryside,
my father sold the bicycle,
the glass-front bookcase,
and the small wooden horse I had ridden as a child.

I cried as I watched those things carried away.
My father scolded me—not harshly,
but with a steady, sobering firmness:

"Don't cry. Things are just things.
As long as we are alive,
we can always start again."

He paused, then added,

"Zeng Guofan was a Hunanese like us.
He lost battle after battle,
and more than once wanted to throw himself into the
river.
But he held on.
In the end, he put down the Taiping Rebellion.

Life will press on you.
You must endure it.

Even with a mountain on your chest,
you must learn to stand."

I have carried those words all my life.

Childhood

A childhood, gray and heavy,
left me breathless.
The drumbeats outside the door
tightened my heart in waves—
Were the Red Guards coming again
to raid our home, denounce us, burn the books?

On our first day of exile,
we carried plump, white steamed buns—
and the hungry village children followed us, staring.
Within a year,
I had become one of them.

Verdant hills and flowing streams—
a land so fertile,
yet unable to sustain
its living souls.

By the dim kerosene lamp,
I read and wrote.
My mother would whisper,
"Kerosene is too dear—sleep now.
You must rise early tomorrow."

On moonlit nights,
a soft wind stirred,
cicadas cried endlessly in the trees.
I would look up at the stars
and dream that one day
I would walk out of those mountains
and see the world beyond.

When the Cultural Revolution ended,
I was admitted to university.
The shadows of childhood did not disappear,
but "going abroad" became the distant hope
I quietly clung to.

I was rejected twice by the U.S. Embassy.
The third time, on the train to Beijing,
I told myself:
If it doesn't work this time,
I will stop trying.

But that was the time
I received a scholarship to Ohio University.

At the visa interview,
a young American officer reviewed my documents and

said,
"Your parents are in the U.S. Your sister is in the U.S."

My heart sank.
I thought, *It's over. He'll assume I plan to immigrate.*

But unexpectedly, he smiled.
"Well," he said,
"I'm going to approve your visa anyway."

He signed the form
and slid a slip of paper toward me.
"Come back in three days to pick up your passport."

I could hardly believe what I heard.
When I walked out of the building,
joy, exhaustion, and relief collided inside me,
and tears came uncontrollably.

People watched me,
but no one spoke.

The sun was bright.
I walked slowly along Xiushui East Street,
noticing its beauty for the first time.
For the first time in years,
I breathed fully, deeply,
without weight pressing on my chest.

I thanked God—
though at the time,
I did not yet know Him.

Now I understand:
He had already been guiding my steps.
He had not given me burdens I could not bear.

I once thought faith would turn suffering
into a memory left behind.

But now I see:
The true *exodus*
is not simply crossing a border on a map.

It is stepping out of fear.
Rising out of hopelessness.
Facing God—
and facing one's own heart.

So I ask myself, quietly:

Have I truly come out of Egypt at all?

Chapter 7 · The Shift of Position

Introduction: The Place of Departure

I once asked myself, *"Have I truly come out of Egypt?"*
There was no answer.
But the question settled in me like a seed—quiet,
hidden, slowly taking root.

Some people travel thousands of miles and never really
depart.
Some steps look steady, yet only circle around fear.
The true exodus is not a change of geography.
It is the movement of the heart—
from fear to trust,
from avoidance to dependence,
from what appears successful in the eyes of others
to what is obedient in the eyes of God.

In time, I came to understand that what God was asking
me to leave

was not merely that office—
but the place in my heart
where survival had quietly replaced faith.

For many years, I believed that *leaving* was the same as
being free.
But true departure is never escape—it is a choice.

I began reading the Old Testament again, not seeking
miracles,
but watching the people themselves—
people who hesitated, stumbled, complained, regretted,
and yet kept walking.
They were not saints.
They were human.
They were me.

Their stories reflected my own.

I never imagined that after all it took to come to
America—
earning a master's degree, working for years to establish
a place—
I would stand again at a crossroads.

Reality does not wait until we feel ready.
It arrives, and demands a response.

I thought of Esau who traded his birthright for a bowl of
stew.

And I asked myself:
Was this job, this position, my bowl of stew?

As believers, wherever we stand, we are called to look to God and trust Him.
He is faithful.
He leads His people out of difficult places.

So I went to the finance director and told her my concerns about the accounts.
She listened quietly, then said:

"I pray for the company every day.
But even after praying, I still don't know what the right thing is."

She hesitated before continuing:

"The boss says the company supports over a hundred families.
Rules are rigid; people are living.
The payments all go into the proper accounts.
The bank doesn't lose anything.
In business, sometimes you need special means.
God has blessed us—that's why we've come this far.
I take that as His answer.
So I have peace."

I did not argue with her.
I simply prayed for clarity.

In the weeks that followed, the conviction quietly grew within me:
Go.

I did not yet know where I would go.
But I knew I could not stay.
I had to come out of Egypt.

I told my sister and the finance director.
My brother-in-law questioned me:

"You don't have another job yet. Why resign now?"

I replied,

"Because I want to experience God's protection and provision—not just for myself, but so the boss may see that God is alive, our true source."

He frowned.
"That sounds like testing God."

I shook my head.

"If I were to throw myself off a building and say, 'If God is real, He will save me,' that would be testing Him.
But this is different.
This is walking by faith.
'Without faith it is impossible to please God.' (Hebrews 11:6)"

I thought of the Book of Joshua:
The Jordan River did not part first.
It parted only after the priests stepped into the water.

**Faith is never waiting for the storm to clear.
Faith is stepping forward in the rain.**

During my final week at the company, I began sending
out résumés.
On Friday, as I walked out of the office for the last time,
the willow branches swayed gently in the breeze.
A quiet ache rose in me.

This had been my workplace for years; everything was
familiar.
To begin again meant starting from nothing.

In that moment, I understood something of how
Abraham must have felt when he left Ur of the
Chaldeans—
no visible guarantee in hand,
only a call that could not be seen.

To step forward without certainty is a deep spiritual
practice.
But Scripture says, "Perfect love casts out fear."

If we love God with all we are,
He will lead us over mountains
and into freedom.

During the first week after I resigned, I received an
interview invitation from a Jewish-owned company.
A week later, I was hired.

God is faithful.
When we look to Him, He guards our hearts and minds
and guides our steps onto the path of peace.

I knew this was not the end.

"Coming out of Egypt" is never merely resigning from a
job,
moving to a different place,
or changing direction.

It is a farewell that happens in the soul—again and
again.
A quiet awakening—again and again.
A choosing to trust God—
not because everything is clear,
but because I am willing to believe.

I was never without fear.
I simply learned to walk while afraid.

I once trembled at the sound of drums.
I once made promises under the stars.
And now, I stand again at the edge of a river—
not knowing whether the waters will part,
not knowing whether I will reach the other side.

But I know this:

**There is the God who once parted the Red Sea
for me.
He will lead me across the Jordan as well.**

I did not leave the company because I had all the
answers.
I left because I learned this:

When I cannot see, I can still believe.
When I cannot control, I can still obey.

So I am not simply someone who left a job.
I am someone who is coming out of Egypt—
someone who chooses, in the face of success and desire
and fear,
to follow the faint light that remains.

The light is soft,
but it is there.
And it calls me forward—
one step,
and then another,
toward what I do not yet know.

The Choice of Endurance

Introduction

The world thinks of choice as a race,

a striving,

a way to rise above the clamor of many voices.

But on the spiritual journey,

the deepest choices

are often hidden in endurance—

not in rushing forward,

but in standing still;

not in proving oneself,

but in quietly trusting the One who calls.

True endurance

is not mere willpower,

but the surrender that makes room

for God's life to dwell within.

Only in emptiness

can His fullness come;

only in endurance

can His lifting hand be found.

This is not an escape from reality,

but a space carved out within reality,

where eternal light breaks through,

and a humble vessel

becomes His dwelling of glory.

Chapter 1 · A Father's Fury

Introduction

Some flames burn away expectation,

and some silences give birth to faith.

True defiance

is not in loud debate,

but in choosing gentleness when denied,

in holding fast to love when misunderstood.

For endurance

is not about winning applause,

but about answering the love

of the One who calls—

faithfully holding, even in the smallest places,

the trust He has entrusted.

The rice cooker steamed in the kitchen,

and the pot of pork rib soup boiled over, filling the air with fragrance.

My father stood at the doorway, his face twisted as if he had swallowed bitter medicine,

and hurled a sentence like a stone:

"You are the most useless person I have ever seen."

The air turned cold in an instant.

The soup kept bubbling, but it could not dissolve the heaviness that settled in the room.

It was 1995. I worked as a junior accountant in a Jewish company.

The job was light, the pay meager.

Computers were in their golden age.

My father urged me to study programming; I shook my head.

"Then take the CPA exam," he pressed.

But I would need extra credits—working by day, studying by night.

Who would stay with my daughter then?

I could not trade her childhood for money,

or push her into the loneliness most feared by children of a single parent.

His words cut like a knife, one after another:

"You refuse computers, you refuse the CPA exam. What exactly do you want?

Do you plan to play with your child for the rest of your life? Look at your sister—

even with an English degree she can program.

And you, with mathematics, do not even dare to try.

I knew you were useless, but I did not think you could fall this low!"

I lowered my head and ladled soup into a bowl.

The steam rose, but could not soften the fury etched between his brows.

Since childhood, his standards had been as high as a mountain I could not climb.

The words I heard most often were, "You are stupid,"

sometimes sharpened with, "Stupider than a pig."

Over the years, those words became background noise.

I learned to endure, to let them pass.

But to my sister, he was another man—

indulgent, doting, rarely demanding.

That day, I did not argue.

After coming to faith, I had learned to lean elsewhere.

Quietly, I said to him:

"Give me some time. You will see the result.

What God gives us is always beyond what we ask or imagine."

Amid the rising steam,

it was the first time I spoke such certainty before him.

Later, when my daughter went to college and then to work,

we saw each other less.

But my heart held no regret—

in the years when she needed me most, I was there.

Time and presence cannot be replaced by money.

That endurance became the witness of my faith—

not to win on the stage of the world,

but to quietly keep the love God entrusted.

True success is not in what heights you reach,

but in whether, even in the smallest places,

you still hold His trust.

Chapter 2 · Jacob, the Limping One

Introduction

Some blessings

are not gained in the running,

but revealed in the limp left after the struggle.

True transformation

is not by human striving,

but in the emptying,

where God's life comes to dwell.

Fate cannot foretell the future,

nor can a license define one's worth—

only the God who waits at the ford of Jabbok

gives a new name in the place of weakness,

and mends eternity through the cracks.

Spring turned to summer.

The company's performance lagged, and salaries froze.

My father, seeing no progress in my career, grew ever sharper in his words.

His generation poured their unfulfilled ambitions into their children—

career first, family second,

like Yu the Great who passed his own door three times but never entered.

Yet I knew in my heart:

a life without roots drifts like duckweed.

Home gives roots, and with roots, branches can spread and bear fruit.

After coming to faith, I learned to lean on God:

"The world and its desires pass away, but the one who does the will of God lives forever." (1 John 2:17)

"Look at the birds of the air; they do not sow or reap... yet your heavenly Father feeds them." (Matthew 6:26)

I told my father: God is real and living.

He replied coldly, "You've lost your mind."

It was as if an unseen river divided us:

on one shore, his fate and fortune;

on the other, my faith.

His severity had once shaped my resilience.

So when I read Jacob's story, my heart was stirred.

I too was one who strove.

By nature I had learned to contend, never yielding;

yet in the spirit I longed to surrender.

I longed for God's life to dwell within me.

At OU, I entered the library at dawn and returned home
at night.

But on Sundays, I slept in and missed worship.

My sister was the opposite: she slept through weekdays,

yet rose early on the Lord's Day.

Often she nodded off during service,

unable to recall the sermon afterward.

In people's eyes, she seemed careless;

yet God treasured even that small willing heart,

and her whole life was blessed.

Through her I understood:

what God values is not human striving,

but a heart turned wholly toward Him.

For the weakness of God is stronger than men,

and the foolishness of God is wiser than men.

When my father was young, he had our family's fortunes told.

The record book is still preserved.

The accuracy of those predictions once shook me.

I even carried a 24-karat golden Guanyin pendant,

but it could not give me peace.

Until Scripture entered my heart:

the God of Abraham, Isaac, and Jacob showed me

that both history and the future rest in His hand.

I burned the fortune-telling book,

removed the idols,

and followed Him alone.

Then I understood:

the true choice is not chasing outward "powers,"

but clinging to the God who calls me, even in the dark.

I didn't become a CPA.

Instead, I became an "Israel"—

named through my limp,

blessed in my weakness.

My father's silence was the sigh of a generation;

my endurance became the turning of another.

Not fate, not licenses,

but the God who feeds the birds

stitched up my broken places with His own hand.

Like Ruth gleaning in the fields,

like Jacob limping into blessing—

this is my faith:

not escape,

but holding fast to eternity within reality.

Chapter 3 · The Light of Companionship

Introduction

The world believes glory comes from titles,

yet God hides glory in the faint light of companionship.

True choice

is not about rising to high positions,

but about whether one is willing, in the most ordinary moments,

to be emptied,

to make room for love.

Companionship is not surrender,

but a spiritual persistence—

holding gentleness in poverty,

holding presence in busyness,

holding the lamp that never goes out

amid the temptations of the world.

My daughter loved to eat. On Friday afternoons we went to restaurants during half-price hours; on Saturdays, to a cheap buffet, then to the half-price bookstore.

I remember one winter day, the flags outside snapped in the wind as we pushed open the restaurant door. Warm air and fragrance rushed toward us. Halfway through the meal, she looked up, smiling:

"Life is so good."

My heart ached.

What I could give her was so little—discounted clothes, second-hand books, meals at half price.

Yet she smiled as if the whole world were in that moment.

A child's heart is simple; the smallest gift can satisfy.

I said nothing, only touched her head.

The sun was bright that day; we sang as we drove home.

Happiness, in truth, is simple.

By then she was in ninth grade, with a list of classics to read each week.

My English was still not strong, so I used the chance to read with her.

We sat side by side in the living room, reading and discussing, then I asked her to write reflections.

Whenever I read her words, I paused.

The feelings were familiar, but she expressed them in English with clarity and depth.

What I could only sketch, she captured sharply.

Looking at her young face, I thought: Is this truly my daughter? How can she have such insight?

At that moment, I knew she had grown.

She loved to sing. Whenever she was home, the house rang with melody.

At night her room fell quiet, leaving only steady breathing.

I gently closed her door and returned to my desk.

The lamp's light was dim, but tender—shining on her homework, shining on my ledgers.

Once she rubbed her eyes and came in:

"Mom, do you often stay up so late?"

I smiled and nodded. "Mm. When I finish these, others will save much time tomorrow."

She gave a faint "Oh," half understanding, and closed the door.

By day, I was the most ordinary worker in the accounting department;

by night, I checked every figure to the smallest detail.

No certificate, no title—yet I knew every number must be exact.

Perhaps the world prizes positions.

But what she needed was a mother wholly present.

As for the future, I did not know.

I only wished to guard the present.

I thanked the Lord that in this world of restless desire,

I could still remain quiet in heart—

to be with her, to read, to think,

and not be enticed by gain.

Sometimes I wondered: what had I given up?

Titles, promotions, the world's "success."

But I knew it was not loss—it was emptying.

Emptying anxiety, vanity, the urge to control,

to make room for God's light,

for my daughter's laughter,

for His dwelling in our small home.

To accompany is to be emptied.

And emptying is not nothingness, but preparation—

a space for His love to flow,

for His life to grow.

To read and speak with her, to witness her growth—

what could be better than this?

This light was not only the lamp's glow,

but the light of God,

shining on her growth,

shining on the path I walked in endurance.

Chapter 4 · The Unexpected Lifting

Introduction

Some steps are not climbed one by one,

but suddenly appear beneath your feet—

bringing both surprise and trembling.

For you know, the hand that lifts you

is not your own,

but the God who sees your quiet labor.

Lifting is not a reward,

but a trust;

not the end of glory,

but the beginning of witness.

That dim lamp had kept me company through countless nights.

Its light shone on my daughter's homework,

and on the rows of numbers I checked again and again—

quiet, meticulous, never meant for anyone to notice.

Until the day news spread through the office:

the Controller had handed in his resignation.

I stayed at my desk,

turning page after page of the month-end reports,

checking every line.

My heart was calm—

such personnel shifts felt far beyond my reach.

By my third year at the Jewish company,

my title was still "staff accountant."

Yet my work had long surpassed the title.

As the Controller's assistant,

nearly every account passed through my hands before reaching his signature.

He was strict, demanding precision.

I had grown used to his silent gaze,

making correction after correction until the numbers were seamless.

Gradually, he entrusted me with the most critical accounts.

By all logic, his seat should have gone to one of the two managers.

Both held CPA licenses, both had stronger credentials.

I never once put myself on the list.

No license, no application, no pursuit—

I only thought: it is enough to do the work at hand.

Days later, the CFO called me into his office.

He said directly, "I intend for you to take the Controller's role."

I froze. "Me? But—"

He smiled. "I've seen your work these three years.

You know the system,

and you keep the books clean.

This seat fits you better than anyone else."

In that moment, what rose in me was not pride, but reverence.

By human rule, I was unqualified;

by God's grace, the place was given.

Silently, I prayed:

"Lord, this is not mine to deserve.

If You set me on high,

let me not forget You there."

I thought of Ruth—

she only gleaned in the fields,

yet was blessed by Boaz's favor.

From the day I became Controller,

my father never scolded my career again.

Once, he told his friends with a laugh:

this was the fruit of years of "strict discipline."

I only smiled, without dispute.

In his laughter there was pride,

but also a veil—

as if he could finally lay aside his anger.

But I knew well:

the honor was not his,

nor mine,

but God's.

Yet God's grace does not mean calm seas forever.

Sometimes He places a person on high

not to shield them from the storm,

but to make their witness shine all the clearer within it.

The joy of promotion had scarcely faded,

when a new tempest,

already gathering unseen,

drew me into its very center.

Chapter 5 · The Battlefield of Grace

Introduction

Grace is not an end, but a new frontline.

It is not always flowers and applause;

sometimes it is questioning eyes,

silent struggles,

and tears and prayers behind a thousand pages of law.

True victory is not about defeating someone,

but about keeping, in tightening days of trial,

a heart upheld by God.

For to endure on the battlefield

is to contend within grace—

not by one's own strength,

but by the Lord who never misses His time,

even in the storm.

When the Controller appointment was announced, not everyone was pleased.

The accounting manager, holding her CPA license and with seniority above mine,

believed the seat was rightfully hers.

She went straight to the CEO, accusing the CFO of unfairness.

The CEO only replied quietly:

"I trust his judgment."

With one short sentence, all her hopes were shut.

A year later she resigned, and took the company to court,

accusing it of racial discrimination.

While the lawsuit dragged on, I faced a new challenge—

the CPA exam.

After my daughter entered college, I finally had time.

To fill my credits, I enrolled in a summer law course.

The textbook was over a thousand pages thick.

Days at work, evenings in class, weekends buried in study.

Multiple-choice questions repeated endlessly, draining my strength.

On the day of the final exam, driving to campus,

my heart was heavy.

If one school exam was this hard,

how could I ever face the CPA?

Tears brimmed in my eyes.

Then the car radio spoke with sudden clarity:

"Do not weep, do not be afraid. I am your God, and I will keep you."

I froze—was this for me?

Surprise turned to tears.

It was the cry of being comforted by God Himself.

At my lowest valley, He steadied my faith again.

With my law course complete, I turned to CPA prep.

Four subjects at once—accounting, auditing, taxation, law—

four mountains standing tall before me.

I made a strict plan: full-time work by day, study by night,

weekends hardly leaving home.

On exam day, I rose before dawn to pray,

reviewed the key points, then hurried to the test site.

Two days, four subjects.

There were many hard questions,

but within me was a quiet assurance:

though I am limited, His grace is enough.

Months later, the results came:

all four passed at once.

Tears flowed again—this time, tears of gratitude.

The burden lifted, the path ahead seemed brighter.

The colleague's lawsuit slowly faded,

the storm in the workplace settled.

When my father heard I had passed the CPA,

he was overjoyed.

With brush and ink he wrote a scroll:

The sun sets behind the mountains, the Yellow River flows to the sea.

To see a thousand miles farther, one must climb a thousand feet higher.

And he inscribed:

"Life's pursuit has no end; beyond one peak lies another,

beyond one sea lies another.

Shan, having conquered the CPA exam in one battle,

I write with joy, your father's hand."

Looking back now,

those years were not about what I achieved,

but about what God kept me from losing:

I did not lose the tenderness of being a mother.

I did not lose the steadfastness of faith.

I did not lose the heart to accompany.

Not every choice wins applause.

But every choice made for love and faith

is remembered in heaven.

I do not know how many mountains and seas still lie ahead.

But I know this:

wherever I go,

the God who comforted me in the valley,

and upheld me on the heights,

will be with me still.

This is not a book about success,

but about endurance.

Endurance in unseen corners,

endurance in nights of tears and prayer,

endurance in each choice

to answer the love of the One who calls.

I have been silent in workplace storms,

wept under exam pressure,

wandered in family moves,

and doubted in seasons of dryness.

Yet in every valley,

God never left.

Through a word on the radio,

an unexpected comfort,

a family member's encouragement,

He steadied my path again.

I do not write for those who have "arrived,"

but for those still struggling, still waiting.

May you see your own reflection in these words,

and hear God's gentle call.

May you know—

you are not alone,

you are not dismissed,

you are not forgotten.

You are remembered by God Himself,

and in your weakest place,

He will show His strength.

Endurance is not retreat,

but walking forward.

Prayer

Lord,

You are the God who is never late in the storm.

You not only comfort me in the valley,

but also uphold me on the heights.

You know my fears and my unworthiness,

yet You still place the steps beneath my feet,

that I may stand in grace—

not for glory,

but to keep walking on.

May I not lean on my own understanding,

nor be swayed by human applause,

but look only to You—

the Lord who gives life, who grants victory,

and who prepares the way.

May I, on every new battlefield,

still keep the heart upheld by You.

In the name of Jesus Christ I pray,

Amen.

In those days of endurance,

God remembered my small choices

and granted me promotion in the workplace.

Life was no longer poor,

and my heart overflowed with gratitude.

Yet the human heart is often this way:

in want, it seeks urgently;

in plenty, it grows slack.

I thought I could go on in peace,

but without knowing it, I drifted into sleep again.

It was in such comfort

that God led me into another journey—

a migration, a long road.

There I came to see:

unless one abides in Him,

even outward success cannot save the soul from dryness.

And so begins the next story—

"The Year of Migration: From Desire to Connection."

The Year of Migration: From Desire to Connection

Grace in Weariness, Turning Back in Silence

Chapter Introduction | John 15:5

"I am the vine; you are the branches.

If you remain in me and I in you, you will bear much fruit;

apart from me you can do nothing."

Cleveland—a city once built on steel—had long fallen quiet after industry declined. Though it still boasted championship teams, a renowned symphony, and world-class hospitals, its economy had collapsed, leaving it one of the poorest cities in America. Young people left and rarely returned—unless they were studying medicine.

In the fall of 2009, my daughter came home for Thanksgiving. Standing in the kitchen doorway with a freshly washed apple in her hand, she said almost casually, "Mom, why don't you move closer to us? We're so busy—it's hard to come home even once a year."

She spoke lightly, as though in passing. Yet to me her words felt like a kite string pulled taut. Ever since she left for college, she had been drifting farther and farther away, like a kite carried by the wind. I no longer wished to tug her back, only to draw near—to see her a little more, to keep her company a little longer.

I nodded, though unease stirred within me.

When I told my younger sister, she urged me on. "Housing prices have dropped these past two years. You can still afford a place in Virginia. If you wait too long, it may be too late."

And so, in 2010, past the age of fifty, I began the migration—selling a house, buying another, changing jobs, starting over.

The old saying proved true: *even in later years, strength can be renewed.*

March in Cleveland still felt like winter. Snow lingered along the driveways, as though the city itself refused to wake from a long dream. After work, I came home to pack and sort, discarding bag after bag of things I had once clung to. Memories, too, were sealed away like boxes—layer upon layer folded into the suitcase of the past.

The house sold quickly. On signing day, I stood in the empty living room. Half my heart felt lightened; the other half was filled with the unknown future.

In April, during a company holiday, I stayed a few days at my daughter's. On the day I left, a realtor showed me a small house. Sunlight poured into the living room, and without hesitation I said, "I'll take it."

The decision came like the first breeze of spring—not asking about direction, only about warmth.

Days later, I received an interview notice and flew back to Virginia. The meeting was held in a café in Vienna. The weather was clear, the streets crowded with traffic, the air alive with spring. The interview went smoothly, and soon I was offered the job. It felt as though God had answered every detail of my prayers.

I thought, *this is God's blessing.*

But on the first day of work, I discovered what I had overlooked:

The office was far—far too far—from home.

I lived in Fairfax, Virginia, while my new job was in Southeast Washington, D.C., near the Maryland border. No metro line reached it, and buses were unreliable. Driving was my only option. I-66, I-495, I-395—traffic jams everywhere, the streams of cars like a river that would not yield. Each commute was two and a half hours one way. More than twenty-five hours a week disappeared on the road.

Weariness clung to me like a shadow. I no longer had energy to read Scripture, nor time to join church gatherings. Life became like a car stuck on the highway—engine running, yet going nowhere.

Regret followed me: Why hadn't I asked about distance? Why hadn't I prayed more carefully?

Looking back, I realized my prayers had been filled with *me*:

I wanted to move.

I wanted to be near my daughter.

I wanted a new job.

I had never once asked, "Lord, what is Your will?"

And He had never interrupted me.

Step by step, my prayers pressed forward. Step by step, He let me have my way.

He was silent—yet in that silence He waited for me to awaken.

His silence was not abandonment, but mercy's patient watch.

I, however, was often a loud person. As a child in Wuhan, our house stood beside the railway. Every hour the trains thundered past, shaking the walls. My father was hard of hearing, so we always raised our voices at home. Over time, loudness became second nature.

In America, I slowly learned to "empty" myself—even my voice had to learn restraint. Each morning at work, my first reminder was always: *Speak softly today.*

My upbringing had given me a booming voice; my faith journey was teaching me to find quiet within it.

Half a year later, I finally found another job, closer to home. Not because I was wise, but because God did not leave me to dry up completely.

He still led me, still showed His kindness.

Reflection

In those days, I often asked myself:

Had my decision to move truly been a mistake?

If it was born only out of my own desire, why did God still open the way?

Only later did I begin to understand:

His leading does not always run straight into blessing.

Sometimes it takes the long road, through detours and wilderness.

What looks like failure in human eyes may, in God's eyes, be pruning.

He allowed me to stumble in weariness—

not to drive me to despair,

but so that in the dryness I might learn more deeply:

apart from Him, all my striving is but an engine idling in place.

Human beings are a strange creation.

Even after the "Exodus" of faith's high moments, one can fall swiftly into the valley.

Even after making "choices of endurance," one can grow loose and weary, detached from the vine.

I once thought a single spiritual encounter could sustain me for life.

I forgot it was only one watering, not a lasting connection.

A branch that does not remain daily in the vine will wither,

even if yesterday it bore fruit in abundance.

We often imagine that victory is the end of faith.

But true life is not a one-time watering; it is a daily abiding.

Bethlehem's bread must be received day by day,

or else the soul will die in Jericho's dust.

And spiritual victories, if not rooted in the Lord, soon fade into yesterday's memory.

At last, I understood:

Too many of my prayers had been filled with *I, I, I*—

the cries of a child at the breast,

hungry for grace, but not yet clinging to the Lord Himself.

They were words of faith, but not yet the life of faith.

The Lord is not the executor of my wish list.

He is the Vine, and I am a branch.

Without abiding in Him, I am nothing more than a severed twig—

shouting prayers, yet unable to bear fruit.

True blessing is not measured by smooth days,

but by unbroken communion with Him,

by a heart that learns to be quiet enough to hear His will.

So I began to release my "What do I want?"

and to ask instead:

"Lord, who do You want me to become?

How do You want me to remain in You?"

In this city of endless traffic, in this life of weariness,

I long to be joined to Him again—

as a branch joined to the Vine.

No longer a spiritual infant,

but one who abides, who bears fruit,

and whose life brings glory to His name.

Closing Prayer · Returning to the Vine

Lord,

I once thought that choosing the right path

would lead me into fields of blessing.

Yet in days hemmed in by endless traffic,

I came to see—apart from You, I cannot take a single step.

You never reproached me;

You only kept silent watch,

waiting until I reached the end of my own desires.

Lord,

I no longer ask You to fulfill my plans;

I ask only that I return to Yours.

Let me be still, like morning dew

resting upon the leaf of Your mercy.

Let me be soft, like a branch upon the Vine,

not striving, not boasting,

only drawing life from You.

If You do not lead me, I dare not take a step.

If You do not dwell in me, I have no strength.

Awaken me with the breeze of Your Spirit.

Root me with the tendrils of Your love.

Plant me deeply, wholly,

to live in You, to abide in You.

In You,

I am no longer a drifting kite,

but a branch, a home,

a vessel beloved by You.

In the name of Your Son, Jesus Christ, amen.

Transition

The footsteps of migration taught me this:

apart from the Lord, I am nothing more than a wandering kite.

But once joined again to Him,

He placed me in a new environment,

where I began to learn to walk alongside those of different backgrounds.

In a workplace veiled with mist,

He did not leave me to stumble alone,

but arranged fellow travelers—

to share light, to watch over one another.

And that is the story of the next chapter—

"Light, Walking Through the Fog."

Light, Walking Through the Fog

General Introduction · Light in the Fog

We all walk in the fog—

the fog of systems, the fog of history,

the fog of identity, the fog of gender.

They cloud our direction

and blur the faces we carry.

Yet still, there are those who choose to shine.

Not to be seen,

but to cast a small light upon the path beneath their feet,

so that those who walk beside them

are not entirely lost.

This is not an epic of triumph,

but a testimony of endurance—

of those who keep faith in silence,

who take root in the cracks,

who continue toward the light

even where the fog is thickest.

Their names are Tess, and Anika,

and mine, and yours—

all who still choose to walk forward in the wind.

May this chapter

be a small flame in the fog,

kindling a glimmer for those still on the road—

a light to go on.

Chapter 1 · Beneath the System

Introduction

A system is meant to be the garment of order,

yet so often it veils the true light.

Only those who still choose faithfulness and integrity

within its rigid rules

can keep it from becoming a shackle.

The projects funded by the federal government came
with regulations as clear and stern as commandments
engraved on bronze tablets.

Every disbursement had to be issued within seven working days.

Every transfer required dual verification.

Every contract—its date, amount, and vendor—had to withstand the scrutiny of the auditors' unblinking eyes.

What appeared to be strict procedures was, in truth, a test of human faithfulness.

And it was there that I first saw Tess's quiet radiance.

She always arrived earlier than I did.

Her desk stood by the window, where the morning light fell across her face like a thin layer of gold.

The sound of phones and keyboards intertwined, rising and falling like an hours-long symphony.

She reviewed every funding request submitted by branch offices.

Her notes were concise, her signatures firm and swift.

When the documents reached me, I needed only to confirm them before forwarding everything to accounting for the wire transfers.

Week after week, the funds flowed steadily across the world—sometimes in the millions, sometimes in the tens of millions.

She was fluent in every procedure, her English clear and steady, handling complexity with the ease of water finding its own course.

Yet what I admired most was not her competence, but her inner order.

In work that was fast-paced and high in stakes, she was never flustered, never careless.

At first I thought she was simply calm.

Later I realized—it was steadiness shaped by faith.

Tess was from Ethiopia, around thirty years old.

Her skin was warm brown; she wore no makeup; her long hair was tied neatly into a ponytail.

Her features were not delicate, yet they carried sincerity and quiet grace.

Her voice was gentle, her tone low, naturally inviting trust.

She dressed simply, favoring deep colors, never drawing attention.

She told me of a tradition in her hometown:

Before a woman could marry, she was required to cook for the groom's family.

If the food was unsatisfactory, the engagement was called off.

If it was acceptable but not good enough, she would have to live in the groom's household for a month, learning under the eye of the future mother-in-law.

And if, after a month, the mother-in-law was still displeased—the marriage dissolved.

"That was truly a kind of torment," she said softly.

"Why must a woman endlessly prove she is good enough? A woman's world should not be confined to a kitchen."

I told her about my schooling in a rural Chinese village,

where families believed that daughters would eventually marry out, belonging to another household—

and so many were unwilling to let girls continue their studies.

As women, it seemed we were destined to bear the weight the world placed upon us.

In our conversations, I learned she, like me, was a Christian.

Her salary was far lower than her ability deserved.

For two consecutive years, I fought for a seven-percent raise for her; even so, it remained below the market rate.

I encouraged her to pursue her CPA license.

Within a year, she passed all the exams with excellence.

Riding this momentum, I recommended her for promotion to Finance Manager.

The proposal dropped like a stone into a deep well—no sound, no explanation.

The higher-ups declined, offering no reason, and requiring none.

In that moment, I began to understand:

No matter how clear the process,

no matter how refined the system—

everything, in the end, rests in human hands.

If the heart is closed, the road will not open.

I once believed that leaving my homeland meant crossing an invisible threshold.

Only later did I realize:

the threshold was never in the soil beneath my feet,

but in the human heart itself.

There are things effort alone cannot change.

All I could do was stand still in the wind

and do the work that was mine to do.

So I continued:

I kept the ledgers clean, the procedures steady,

holding a small light for the team

amid the intricate machinery of the system.

The work did not draw attention,

yet it kept the company moving

with a quiet, faithful rhythm

even under the severity of outside scrutiny.

As these thoughts rose within me,

the long-suppressed tides of the heart

unfolded into verse—slowly, quietly—

from deep within.

Life wears us down.

I cannot say when it began—

only that, day by day,

our vigor and our dreaming

have thinned and faded,

until at last

we simply make do,

wrinkled with exhaustion.

And yet,

there are moments we still resist—

still long to lift our wings.

But in the open sky,

the cold currents, the storms,

strike without mercy.

And so,

we waver,

we fall.

On the mountain, wildflowers—

red, white, blue—

flare into exuberant bloom.

A stream in the ravine

moves quietly along.

A crow struts along a branch.

Everything is alive with spirit.

And here,

in this world of vivid color,

we drift,

we wander,

bearing wounds

across our bodies.....

Chapter 2 · Invisible Thresholds

Introduction

The truest threshold is not set above the floor,

but hidden deep within the human heart.

Prejudice is not always malice—

sometimes it is habit,

the neglect too familiar to notice.

To cross over requires more than ability;

it demands the courage

that truth alone can uphold.

From a staff announcement sent by HR, I learned that Mike had been promoted to IT Manager.

He was a white man in his forties, tall and well-built, disciplined in manner.

His face was sharply defined, his shoulders broad, his posture upright; when he walked, he carried a quiet force.

His blue-gray eyes were clear and mild, always touched with a smile.

His clothes were simple, well-fitted, usually in a sporty casual style—clean and orderly.

The IT Director, Bruce, was also a white man in his forties.

He knew little about technology, but he excelled at managing people.

Under his hand, the department ran with perfect order.

Mike was Bruce's friend.

He had majored in English at university and knew almost nothing of IT until he was brought into the department a year earlier.

Sensitive to language, he often said:

"When I hear bad English—broken grammar, wrong syntax—it makes me cringe."

English was his mother tongue, and he was proud of it.

Most of the company's employees came from Asia, Africa, and Latin America.

Their accents were thick, their grammar imperfect.

Yet this time, it was his name written on the promotion list.

A year later, he was promoted again—to Assistant Director of IT.

At that time, I carefully drafted and submitted a recommendation for Tess to be promoted to Finance Manager.

The document listed her achievements over the past three years:

- flawless precision in cash disbursements;

- her independent coordination of wire transfers between international contractors and field offices;

- and her passing of all CPA exams with distinction.

When I handed it in, I was full of confidence.

Surely this time the company would have no reason to refuse.

A week later, the reply came:

"Thank you for the recommendation. Since Tess has no management experience, she cannot be promoted at this time."

I sat at my desk, staring at the letter.

Wasn't this absurd?

Because she was not a manager, she had no subordinates;

yet the lack of subordinates was used as the reason she could not become a manager.

With a single sentence, years of loyalty and excellence were brushed aside.

Tess oversaw the cash flow of all field offices,

and she personally trained every new finance officer.

Whenever a field office replaced staff, it was Tess who conducted one-on-one training online.

Did that not count as management?

This crack in their logic laid bare the bias of the system—

an invisible threshold few could cross.

IT, accounting, and budget departments all fell under the CFO's authority.

Yet under the same leadership, the standards for promotion were utterly different.

The company loudly proclaimed "respect and inclusion,"

with banners of corporate values hung high.

But now I understood: their so-called "inclusion"

was a demand that we keep enduring, keep striving, never asking for fairness.

The only thing truly included was injustice itself.

As a manager, I still had to tell Tess:

"Don't lose heart. Work hard. There will be another chance."

She smiled faintly, as though she had already seen through it all:

"I know you did your best. Don't worry. I'll keep working."

Her voice was calm as always,

yet her eyes shone with the steady light of faith.

That afternoon she returned to her desk,

reviewing that week's funding requests,

her motions as orderly as ever.

This was who she was:

in the vast machinery of the system,

she bore the weight of tasks,

checked numbers, carried burdens,

day after day in silence.

Watching her back, I suddenly thought of the flame in the wilderness that does not go out.

She was not promoted, yet she was not defeated.

In the thick fog and the cold machinery of power,

she kept her gaze bright with faith and walked on.

Like a seed hidden in the crevice of stone—

not striving for brilliance,

only rooting itself deeper against the wind.

Chapter 3 · Storms at the Beginning

Introduction

Some storms do not come to destroy,

but to reveal what is real within us.

The immigrant's journey is both wandering of the feet

and a long-distance race of the soul.

In the night, a voice—faint yet unextinguished—
whispers:

"I have always been here."

And so the storm becomes more than storm.

That night, I could not sleep.

The ceiling light was long extinguished,

only the pale glow of the computer screen lingered on
the desk.

In my inbox, that single sentence—

"She has no management experience"—

struck my heart again and again,

like a stone sinking heavily.

In that moment, I understood deeply:

between freedom and equality

there still lay a chasm hard to cross.

America had seemed like a lighthouse in the night,

drawing people from every shore.

That light stood for democracy, freedom, equality, hope.

For its sake we crossed mountains and waters,

left behind what was familiar,

came alone to this strange and wondrous land,

beginning a journey both uncertain and hard.

Years later I realized:

"freedom" here was never simply given—

it was won by the struggles and sacrifices of those before us.

And "equality"

remains a race still unfinished.

Every silent, steadfast soul like Tess

lays one more stone upon its foundation.

Every rejection like hers

reminds us the road is not yet done.

What sustains us to go on

is hope, is faith.

Yet in the stillness of night, I often asked myself:

If I had known how hard this path would be,

would I have stepped on it so resolutely?

During the Cultural Revolution, I was sent with my parents to the countryside.

That summer, at fifteen, I toiled under the blazing sun
for twelve hours in the fields.

At dusk, I hoisted baskets of rice upon a shoulder pole,

walking the narrow ridges with the grain-delivery team,

bringing public grain to the commune station.

Those days were poor and bitter.

I once thought I had tasted all the world's hardship.

But years later, with fifty dollars in my pocket,

I set foot alone in a foreign land.

Only then did I understand:

in this abundant country,

poverty is not just an empty wallet—

it is a life hemmed in at every turn.

The struggle of an immigrant's life

was deeper, lonelier,

than the labor of my youth in the village.

The road of the first generation

is uncommonly hard.

In 1989, I came to study at Ohio University.

It was in Athens, a small town of four seasons,

with its courses divided by quarters.

Scholarship carried me through my studies.

Each term I had to complete sixteen credits,

with grades no lower than a B—

else the funding would be withdrawn.

Nearly all my time was spent in the library:

reading, writing papers, preparing for exams.

That year, I was like a bow drawn taut, never daring to slacken.

After my first accounting class, I went to the professor with questions.

He could not understand my English.

Bluntly, he advised:

"Drop your class."

I left without protest.

His blackboard notes were clear, his calculations precise.

Though I could not follow his lectures,

through pre-study and his chalkboard, I grasped it all.

After the first exam, he was astonished:

the only perfect score in class was mine—

the student he had once advised to quit.

Mathematics had been my undergraduate major.

Anything with numbers, I excelled;

anything with words, I struggled.

Yet I strained with all I had,

and graduated with a 3.67 GPA.

I majored in International Affairs,

with several courses in Accounting.

But reality poured cold water quickly.

Had I been a citizen,

with International Affairs I might have sought a post at
the State Department.

But I was not.

In accounting, with no degree, no license,

doors were shut.

"No way in"—

those words I finally came to know.

This land of freedom felt to my feet

strange and cold.

To study accounting again required tuition I could not
afford.

With the future uncertain, confidence drained,

I began to doubt my worth.

I had fled political oppression,

yet here in the free air

I could find no place to stand.

That contrast shadowed me like a cloud.

For survival, I washed dishes in a Chinese restaurant.

The work was filthy and hard—

taking out garbage, peeling chicken skin.

The trash bins were taller than me.

To empty them, I had to lift buckets overhead,

careful not to be crushed by their weight.

One slip, and waste water would pour down on me.

I cleaned it silently, swallowing my pride.

What I felt was not only dirt and fatigue,

but the heaviness of dignity pressed into the trash.

Later I found work at a motel front desk,

at $4.25 an hour—the minimum wage.

I worked two jobs a day, seven days a week,

enduring by sheer strength.

At times I looked into the mirror,

and asked quietly:

Why did I come to America?

Was it to survive on minimum wage?

The hardest part was not the exhaustion,

but the darkness in my heart:

no direction, no path ahead.

Not knowing what effort

might pry open fate's closed gate.

Looking back now, those days were like

trying with all my might to root in foreign soil.

The bitterness was beyond words.

Because I once struggled at the lowest rung,

I learned how silent endurance

can slowly erode dignity.

I often said it was a time of "trading life for money."

That life lasted a year,

until I found work at a Taiwanese-owned firm.

It was there

I came to believe in Jesus.

From that moment, my life found a quiet direction.

It was not a miracle rewriting fate overnight.

It was a faint glimmer in the dark,

teaching me not merely to survive, but to live.

That year felt like a marathon—

exhausting, with no one waiting at the end.

But I came to see:

not every race needs an audience.

Some roads are meant

to bring you face to face with your truer self.

And in those years near drowning,

I heard a voice—gentle yet steady.

Not in my ears, but in my heart:

"I have always been here."

I began to read the Bible.

Its words, like morning dew,

softened the hardness of my soul.

It was not I who found God,

but He who had long been waiting,

until I finally stopped to listen.

It was then I realized:

I was not walking through the storm alone.

I was walking with Him.

Chapter 4 · Walking Together

Introduction

Some roads are never meant to be walked alone.

To walk together is not to be the same,

but to stand side by side in difference;

not a mere overlap of belief,

but a meeting of lives.

In the fog we set out,

carrying our wounds and our hopes,

still willing to draw near to one another.

Lord—my righteous, faithful, and loving Father,

I quiet myself before You,

to listen to Your words,

to behold Your works in Your dwelling place.

Your grace

is like the morning dew,

refreshing me;

like the mountain mist,

surrounding me.

Before me,

You strike down my enemies,

bringing deliverance to Your children.

You are my hope

in times of trouble.

I will sing to You,

I will praise You—

praise for Your righteousness,

Your faithfulness,

Your love.

(Meditation on Isaiah 18)

During that time, I was learning to listen—

not only to the voice of God,

but also to the faint whispers of lives around me,

voices I had once overlooked.

It was then that I moved houses, and the company
relocated too,

leaving me farther from work.

Anika, from the IT department, lived close to me,

and so we began to commute together every day.

Anika was from India, nearly forty years old.

Her complexion held the warm glow of bronze,

with traces of time gently etched upon her face,

adding a sense of calm and steadiness.

Her eyes were large and deep, as though they could see
far,

and in them was the tenderness of a mother.

She was a mother indeed, with a son and a daughter,

and her smile always carried reassurance.

Her long black hair fell smoothly over her shoulders.

She dressed simply, often in soft-colored dresses,

sometimes with fine earrings that swayed gently as she moved.

Every morning at six, before dawn,

we set out in her Tesla through the thin veil of fog.

I sat in the passenger seat, pressing my fingers to the cold window.

She would play Indian classical music—

a sound both strange and distant to me.

"You're dressed lightly today," I remarked once,

pointing to her short-sleeved dress.

It was then I noticed a scar on her right arm.

Not long, but deep.

She smiled faintly. "Oh, that was long ago,"

she said, as lightly as if mentioning a missed TV show.

The road in the fog stretched quiet and straight.

Then she spoke slowly:

"That year, my husband had an affair.

When he learned I was pregnant with our second child,

he forced me to abort.

I refused. At home he shamed me,

telling me I was ugly,

that his lover was beautiful.

Back in India, I had been Hindu.

My brother was a temple priest.

When I called him, even before I mentioned my pregnancy,

he said, 'This is a boy.'

My first child was a girl.

Five months into my pregnancy, the affair ended.

My husband returned home in rage,

taking his anger out on me.

Once, he struck me.

Afraid of falling and harming the baby, I reached out to steady myself—

my arm hit the glass table, and blood poured out.

The child was saved, but I went to the hospital for stitches.

The doctor asked if I had family with me.

I said only my husband.

They gave me a look, and said nothing more."

Silence filled the car.

Only the music continued.

I glanced down at the scar on her arm,

its pale brown trace stark in the morning light.

There were no tears, no bitterness.

"We still live together," she said calmly.

"I never divorced. The children need me."

Then she smiled again.

I nodded gently, unable to speak.

Inside, my heart tightened.

In that moment, I realized—

she was truly strong.

After six years as colleagues,

I had never guessed that behind her steady presence

was such hidden sorrow.

It was then I understood:

in this land of freedom,

some lives survive without ever truly being free.

Yet she stood in the cracks,

guarding the sacredness of life in her own way.

Every day, in those hours on the road,

we came to know each other more deeply.

She told me her husband was twelve years older,

their marriage arranged by a matchmaker.

They had only met once before the wedding.

She was twenty-two, freshly graduated.

A week after their wedding, her husband left for
America.

A year later, she followed.

On her first weekend in the U.S.,

he took her shopping for earrings.

He chose a $50 pair and handed them to her.

She set them down and chose another pair of the same
price.

He said nothing, and paid.

But when they returned home,

that small "defiance" was met with a beating.

He wanted her to remember:

she must obey, never act on her own.

In India, she had majored in computer science.

After coming to the U.S., she soon found work and opened her own bank account.

Yet her husband kept all his account numbers and passwords hidden from her,

while knowing every detail of her finances.

Even her work emails, he would check regularly.

Later, through her work visa, ABC Company agreed to sponsor her green card.

She had joined the company three years before I did.

One day I asked her:

"Does your brother know about your marriage?

Does he know your husband beats you?"

She answered: "He knows.

He advised me not to divorce.

He said he would pray to the Hindu gods,

asking them to make my husband treat me better."

Hearing this, I fell silent.

My chest tightened with sorrow.

Anika was intelligent and capable.

Many Indians spoke English with a heavy accent,

but hers was nearly flawless.

Her fluent English and clear writing

made her a pillar of the IT department.

The company had already secured her green card.

Bruce, the former IT Director, had been promoted to
Vice President,

with Mike taking his place.

One morning on our commute, Anika told me:

"I've been with this company for nine years.

They sponsored my green card back then,

but my position has never changed.

Now that my status is settled,

I'm going to ask Mike for a promotion."

At home she was a silent, restrained wife,

tightly controlled by her husband.

But in the workplace, she stood without fear—

decisive, strong.

I often marveled

that such contradictions could live in one person.

That day, as she drove quietly,

I looked at her profile

and suddenly felt a light within her,

like the first ray of dawn rising in the fog.

She was about to claim a new place for herself—

the fruit of years of silence, endurance, and persistence.

Yet I knew:

not every "ascent" comes from above.

Some are only another weight of bondage.

But some are lifted by love,

fruits born in the freedom of answering a call.

We sat side by side in the car,

the wheels rolling forward.

I looked up at the not-yet-brightened sky,

and prayed softly in my heart:

"Lord,

teach me to discern the deepest grace You give,

and teach me how to walk together,

along the road of Your steadfast love."

Chapter 5 · Light in Silence

Introduction

Silence does not mean surrender;

it is the whisper from the depths of faith.

Light does not need to shout;

it need only be—

in the cracks of a system,

in the posture of persistence,

in the patient timing of God.

The morning fog lay like an unawakened dream, draped over the car windows.

Streetlights still glowed low, their beams threading through the mist,

sketching the quiet pulse of a city not yet awake.

We sat side by side in silence, but not in awkwardness.

A slow jazz tune spun softly in the air.

"I'm going to ask Mike for a promotion today," Anika said suddenly.

Her voice was steady, without hesitation, without seeking approval.

"And if nothing comes of it?" I turned to glance at her.

"—If I don't ask, nothing will come anyway."

At her words, the fog seemed to thin, dawn breaking faintly at the edge of the sky.

I said nothing more, only nodded.

The music played on, silence flowing out the windows, blending with the morning wind.

At the office I saw Tess. She was, as always, the first to arrive,

seated by the window, sunlight painting her profile in pale gold.

The crisp sound of her keyboard rose—

she was already reviewing the week's cash flow.

She did not boast, nor slack.

She lived out order quietly within the cracks of the system—

not in words, but in life.

Like salt, unseen yet indispensable;

like light, unnoisy yet impossible to ignore.

The Lord Jesus said:

"No one lights a lamp and hides it under a bowl.

Instead they put it on its stand, and it gives light to everyone in the house."

Tess, within layers of constraint,

kept her lamp burning quietly, never extinguished.

Whether in endless disbursement processes

or in the cold echoes of rejection,

her faith seeped through like morning light.

That day, I submitted her promotion form once again to the CFO.

Weeks later, on our commute, I asked Anika, "Any hope this time?"

She answered:

"Mike said the CFO told him the company is freezing promotions—

revenues slowing, costs rising."

I nodded. "The CFO told me the same."

Soon after, however, HR announced a new round of promotions.

Anika went straight to the CFO, calm in demeanor:

"I'd like to ask something."

She began at once:

"Why does this company hold different standards for promotions across departments?"

The CFO stiffened, frowned.

"They're not different. Each department has its own constraints, its own budget."

Anika held her ground, her voice even steadier:

"But our department hasn't seen a single promotion in two years.

IT projects keep multiplying. Workloads have tripled."

She paused, then looked him in the eye:

"If you cannot resolve this, then I'll go to HR."

The CFO clearly did not want escalation.

He rushed to say, "Don't be hasty. Let me coordinate. Give me some time."

That day I asked her, "Weren't you afraid, confronting the CFO directly?

Of being fired?"

She smiled faintly:

"I've already prepared to be fired. I'm job-hunting.

But right now IT rests in my hands.

If they let me go, it's their loss."

A few days later, the CFO informed me:

to cut costs, Tess's work would be split among three existing managers,

with someone else to review their outputs.

I felt my heart sink.

Workplace bias is like dust in the air—

silent, unseen, yet permeating every judgment.

Knowing arguments would be useless,

I bore it in silence.

Hearing of an opening in the Internal Audit Department,

led by the Vice President of Legal,

I reached out to her directly.

She was about fifty, a white woman with short blond hair—

decisive, composed.

Her complexion was pale, fine lines etched at her eyes,

her gray-blue gaze sharp yet steady.

Her attire was always simple: dark suits, white blouses, no jewelry,

save a silver watch at her wrist.

Not dazzling in appearance,

yet she carried a quiet authority.

Her words were few but precise,

and when she entered a room, silence followed.

Years of legal training gave her a logical clarity, an emotional restraint.

Only when speaking of "justice" and "principle"

did a fierce warmth rise in her tone.

I spoke to her about Tess.

She listened, then immediately asked her secretary to schedule an interview.

Soon Tess was transferred to Internal Audit.

Anika, at last, was officially promoted to Manager.

Watching Tess leave that day, a sourness rose in me.

Yet she gently comforted me:

"All is from God. What He gives is always the best."

At the time, I could not see "the best."

I only felt she was being pushed aside—

and that I was powerless.

Spring had come, the wind carrying tender green.

Standing at the window, I felt its touch.

And in that moment, I finally understood:

some departures are not a dismissal, but a leading.

Some silences are not weakness, but deeper trust.

Like the light of spring,

not arriving in a night,

but breaking through winter bit by bit.

A verse from the Old Testament rose in my heart,

softly answering my unrest:

"'For my thoughts are not your thoughts,

neither are your ways my ways,' declares the Lord."

And so I knew:

We need only walk in the light.

The rest is His to order.

Who could have guessed?

The VP of Legal treasured Tess greatly,

fighting each year for her advancement.

Step by step, one rung a year,

she rose—

until, within three years, she became Senior Director of Audit and Compliance—

a speed of ascent unheard of in company history.

Later I often recalled that spring.

Tess was "relocated" in silence.

Anika answered with persistence.

And I, though powerless, carried no regret.

Human order often falters.

Systems grow cold.

Yet in the cracks, some still choose to live as light—

not shining because they are seen,

but shining because they believe.

What we call justice delayed

is only justice awaiting its hour.

What we think forgotten

is only repositioned on God's map.

As Scripture says:

"In all things God works for the good of those who love
Him."

We may still walk within limits and inequities,

stumbling, staggering.

But if there is light within,

it will draw us upward—

toward His higher ways.

Overcomers at the Table
with the Lord

Introduction · The Call of the Table

True overcoming

is not silencing the world's clamor,

but answering God's call

from the depths of the soul.

To sit with the Lord

is not a prize of glory,

but a home of love.

That feast is not only for some distant day—

it is the table being set

in our hearts today.

This is a gentle promise:

All who still say "I will" in weakness,

who keep the lamp in the dark,

who endure injustice by faith,

who hear love's knocking in the silence,

who empty themselves that the Lord may fill—

they shall sit with Him.

Not because we are strong,

but because we were bought by His blood,

upheld by His grace,

and led by His love.

Overcoming is a spiritual posture;

the table is His invitation—

not because of our worthiness,

but because of His mercy and faithfulness.

Chapter 1 · The Seven Lamps

Responding to the Church's Prayer

The Lord walks among the lampstands,

calling each church,

knocking on each heart.

He does not come to cast off,

but to kindle—

to light the church,

and to light my heart.

Coldness quenches love;

compromise veils the light;

pride lulls the soul to sleep.

Yet He still walks, still calls, still waits—

not with thunder of judgment,

but with the cadence of restoring grace.

Ephesus · The Lamp of First Love

Lord, I was once zealous,

yet slowly forgot who You are.

You call me back to my first love—

not a passing flame,

but the loyalty that endures beneath the cross.

First love is not the show of beginnings;

it is choosing to follow

when the warmth has cooled.

I return to the place

where You gave Your life for me

and whisper again:

"Lord, I love You."

Smyrna · The Lamp of Endurance

Lord, You never promised to spare me from

suffering,

but to be with me in its midst.

Endurance is not clenched-teeth resolve;

it is quiet trust beneath the cross.

I fear the valley,

yet I will walk with You

until the dawn of resurrection.

Pergamum · The Lamp of Truth

Lord, in confusion and compromise,

You call me to hold the truth.

Truth is not the blade of debate;

it is the silence of Calvary.

Let me not win by volume,

but be guided by Your nail-scarred hand.

Thyatira · The Lamp of Holiness

Lord, You do not demand perfection;

You summon me to be set apart.

Holiness is not escape from the world,

but Your likeness lived beneath the cross.

Refine me—

not for glory,

but to draw nearer to You.

Sardis · The Lamp of Reality

Lord, You see the bustle without

and the barrenness within.

Reality is not self-defense;

it is confessing my emptiness at the cross.

Strip away my veneers,

and rebuild Your life in me.

Philadelphia · The Lamp of Small Strength

Lord, I have no great power,

no wide influence,

yet You commend my little faithfulness.

Small strength is not weakness;

it is still saying "I will" beneath the cross.

With this small light,

let me walk through the door You open.

Laodicea · The Lamp of Fervor

Lord, I once thought myself rich,

yet before You I am poor.

You counsel me to buy gold refined by fire.

Fervor is not a surge of feeling;

it is being kindled at the cross.

Strip off my self-righteous rags,

and clothe me

in garments washed white

by Your blood.

Coda · The Light of the Cross

Lord, light these seven lamps within my heart;

beneath each lamp lies the shadow of the cross—

loyalty, endurance, silence, holiness, reality, small
strength, fervor—

arrayed like stars in the night sky.

Let me be not only an overcomer at the table,

but a companion on the way of the cross:

to deny myself in the everyday

and walk with You.

Kindle me, Lord.

Make me a small light upon Your lampstand,

to illumine the path

You have walked for me.

Chapter 2 · Reading Revelation

Scripture Lead

"Behold, I stand at the door and knock. If anyone hears my voice and opens the door, I will come in to him and eat with him, and he with me.

To the one who conquers I will grant to sit with me on my throne, as I also conquered and sat down with my Father on his throne."

— Revelation 3:20–21

I once thought Revelation was a book full of fire and thunder.

Each time I opened it, it felt like stepping into a furnace.

The call to be a "conqueror" made me tremble—

I was not such a person.

My prayers lacked fire;

my faith wavered;

my steps stumbled again and again.

I feared I would be one left outside the door.

In those nights I closed the Bible

With a heart heavy in discouragement.

Revelation seemed less a promise than a warning;

less a love poem than an iron statute.

"Conqueror"—a title I felt destined never to receive.

Yet even in that fear I kept turning the pages.

One day I reached chapter three and read:

"Behold, I stand at the door and knock..."

In that moment, my heart was struck.

The Lord had not cast me out,

nor come to condemn;

He stood outside the door and knocked.

It was not fire but an invitation;

not judgment but a table set.

I suddenly understood:

conquest is not a prize I must earn,

but an identity given by His blood.

To conquer does not mean never falling;

it means not abandoning hope after a fall—

to treasure love even in the valley.

"For I live, you also will live."

This is the root of conquering —

not what I can accomplish,

but what He has already done.

Now I know: when He stands and knocks,

His hands still bear the nails.

He does not come to ask why I am weak,

but to invite me to sit at the cross—

not because I have conquered,

but because He has conquered for me.

The Promise of the Table

The feast in Revelation is not the platform of the mighty;

it is a table the Lamb sets for the weak.

The table is not earned by my merit,

but extended by His invitation;

it does not depend on my flawlessness,

but on His blood that cleanses.

Before that table no one must prove himself,

and none are cast out in shame.

Seated in the midst

is the One who gave His life for the world—

His hands still bear the marks;

His eyes are full of mercy.

The table is spiritual intimacy—

not a boisterous triumph,

but a quiet belonging.

Not because we deserve it,

but because He is merciful.

Each emptying is preparation;

each repentance is a return;

each "I will" is an answered step toward the table.

My Response

I have learned:

conquest is not held by my clenched hand,

but by His faithful love.

Fear becomes rest;

discouragement turns to hope.

Revelation is no longer merely thunder,

but a love poem—

addressed to me

and to all who will lift their eyes to the Lamb.

Response is not the end

but the beginning;

conquest is not a final crown

but a rhythm.

The rhythm of conquering

is not willpower's grind,

but the soul's emptying:

to lay down self

is to breathe spiritually;

to empty is to prepare the table.

Each "I will" beneath the cross

draws me nearer to sitting with the Lord.

Therefore I can rest and say:

Lord, though I am not a conqueror,

I am willing to walk with you

until the feast.

Chapter 3 · The Continuance of Preparation

Introduction

On the spiritual road, preparation is not a single act,

but a continual posture—

like the slow spread of morning light,

like grain bending in the wind.

We prepare not because we fully know what will come,

but because we choose to watch in the unknown,

to listen in the silence,

to move forward in the soft "Lord, I will."

Preparation is not for glory,

but for not fleeing beneath the cross;

not to prove ourselves,

but to answer His love.

1. Earthly Continuance

I once thought conquest was a final sprint,

tested only at the finish.

The Lord showed me otherwise:

conquest begins today,

in each moment when a door is knocked

and I respond.

When I choose humility over self-righteousness,

repentance over indifference,

and in weakness whisper, "Lord, I will,"

those are the steps of victory.

Victory is not a distant banner;

it is the responses beneath each step—

obedience in the morning dew,

longing at dusk,

and the willingness, beneath the cross's shadow,

to keep walking toward the light.

2. The Soul's Preparation

The conqueror is not born strong,

but is one who repeatedly returns to the blood.

Identity is not something I hang on to,

but what He has purchased for me.

Preparation is not an anxious push,

but the continuation of love.

And love's continuation often begins

with emptying.

As oil must be refilled day by day,

as garments must be kept clean,

so the soul must continually wait.

If I wander away, He calls;

if I fall, He lifts.

In His enduring love,

my heart is being shaped.

Preparation is not panic;

it is waiting encircled by love—

not frantic running,

but quiet belonging.

Under the cross I learn not to rely on myself,

but on the work He has already finished.

3. The Eternal Direction

"To the one who conquers I will grant to sit with me on my throne."

This is the ultimate promise.

Today's preparation is the path toward that day.

Today's tears are seeds of tomorrow's joy;

today's repentance preludes the eternal song.

Lord, I will carry today's tears and songs toward the feast;

I will keep walking in your promise until I sit with you on the throne.

I will say "I will" beneath the cross,

even if my steps falter and my heart wavers.

You have prepared a seat for me—

not on a stage of glory,

but in your self-giving love.

Closure · The Lamb's Banquet

Revelation is not a terror of fire;

it is a knocking of love.

Conquest is not my strength,

but what He has accomplished.

Lord, let me first empty myself,

that I may be a vessel filled with your light and life.

Today's waiting will become eternal praise:

"Salvation belongs to our God who sits on the throne,
and to the Lamb!"

I breathe out—pain, fear, failure, lament;

I breathe in—grace, life, hope, light.

Breathing out is emptying; breathing in is foundation.

Victory is not by my power,

but by His indwelling—

the One who shows perfect strength

in my weakness.

Until that day,

I will sit at the feast with the saints,

and before the Lamb

give all glory and victory back to you.

An Invitation to the Reader

Dear reader,

if you have ever looked up at the stars in the night,

if you have heard a knock in a fissure of your life,

if you have whispered "I will" in weakness,

then you have walked this path with me.

May you not only read

but re-experience—

the love that never leaves,

the Lord who waits at the door,

the Lamb who prepares the table for you.

And may you, on your journey, also say:

"Lord, I will."

And may you, with me,

sit at His table on that day.

Bearing Witness to the Lord:

The Scroll of My Life, Opened by the Lamb

Introduction · The Soul's Sixfold Knocking

The scroll of life

is not a story I have written,

but grace unfolded by Him, page by page.

I once believed that spiritual growth

came from my own choices—

until I discovered:

every turning point was His knock;

every chapter, His imprint.

These are not merely six experiences,

but six responses of the soul —

from being questioned to being led;

from being guarded to being joined;

from being illuminated to being refined.

Six responses,

shaped into six marks beneath the Cross.

Each mark is a spiritual awakening;

each mark, an invitation of love.

He did not compel me to unveil them.

He simply waited in gentleness,

until I said:

"Lord, I am willing."

These six marks

are not the summary of my life,

but the testimony of my soul—

a witness to the God who never leaves nor forsakes,

who, through running and silence,

through wandering and mist,

drew me back, step by step,

into His embrace.

May you, as you read these six marks,

see not only my story,

but hear His question to your soul:

"What do you seek?"

"Will you follow Him?"

"Will you be guarded, joined, and illuminated?"

For He is still knocking,

still waiting,

still unfolding the scroll of my life

in love.

Chapter 1 · The Knocking of the Soul (Six Seals)

Subtitle: Not Written by Me, but Opened by Him

The First Seal · Questioned

Not I who asked Him,

but He who asked me:

"What do you seek?"

I ran, I prayed, I wrestled,

until one tear

fell into His palm.

Only then did I say:

"Lord, I want You—

nothing else,

only You."

The Second Seal · Led

I thought I was fleeing,

yet it was He

who led me out in light.

Not my choice of direction,

but grace itself

laying a path

through the wilderness.

The cross begins here—

from bondage

into freedom.

The Third Seal · Kept

I did not stand

by winning battles.

I was kept

through silence

and prayer.

Peace was not mine to claim.

It was He

who set a shelter for me

in the storm.

The way of the cross—

to learn obedience

in the wilderness.

The Fourth Seal · Joined

Not the shifting of steps,

but the returning of the soul.

Not a pause in passing,

but a joining into eternity.

No longer a drifting kite,

but a branch,

a home,

a vessel beloved of Him.

The cross is not escape,

but entrance—

into deeper belonging.

The Fifth Seal · Illumined

The mist is not loss,

but the backdrop of faith.

Light is not noise,

but the posture of walking together.

His light shines on my steps,

and on those

who strive to live

in the cracks of systems,

still rooting deep.

Companionship is more

than mutual support.

It is recognition

beneath the cross:

you too

are redeemed.

The Sixth Seal · Refined

The light of Revelation

fell on me—

not to shame,

but to heal.

No longer only a writer,

but one refined.

He is not the judge of fire,

but the inviter of love.

The cross refines,

turning weakness

into His testimony.

Conclusion

The six seals are not my achievement,

but His testimony,

unfolded page by page.

I am not the author;

I am the soul He has opened.

Life is not a chapter I have written,

but a story read aloud

in His light.

He is not merely the One who knocks;

He is the Lover

waiting in the depths of time

for a response.

And I—

I am one

awakened by grace,

learning, through His questions,

to answer,

to return,

to be refined.

May the cross not only mark my past,

but shape my witness,

until I sit with You

at the banquet table.

Yet this is not only my story;

it also reflects the condition of all humanity.

Chapter 2 · The Call within Silence

Subtitle: Grace in the Midst of Suffering

Human suffering

did not begin in the heart of God;

it began the moment

humanity turned away from Him.

From the rebellion in Eden,

history entered the path of self-rule:

we chose the tree of knowledge,

but lost the tree of life;

we chose control,

but lost companionship.

And on the very road

where we imagined ourselves in control,

suffering followed close behind.

God did not use suffering as punishment;

He transformed it into a knocking sound:

calling us back through illness,

awakening repentance through war,

inviting prayer through loneliness.

"I stand at the door and knock."

This is not thunder of judgment,

but the whisper of love.

In my devotions

I once read Kings and Chronicles.

The rise and fall of dynasties

was more than political change;

it was a mirror of the spirit.

Humanity repeats the same pattern:

• blessed → forgetting God → self-righteous → falling

• fallen → crying out → delivered → rebelling again

This is not only an ancient story;

it is the cycle of my own life.

In abundance I grew cold,

in drought I cried out,

in crying out I was delivered,

yet in safety I slumbered again.

So I do not speak to condemn humanity,

but to testify:

"I too am the one who rebelled,

yet the Lord still chooses

to open the scroll of my life."

In the days of the Old Testament,

human weakness could not be hidden under the law.

They could not keep the commands;

so history became a lament,

failures gathered into tears,

and tears swelled into rivers of exile.

Yet God did not end with human collapse—

He wove redemption's melody into the lament,

planted a promise of homecoming in the exile.

Until that day

when the Lamb, upon the cross,

fulfilled the law for us.

Grace was no longer distant,

but He Himself came to the table.

We no longer sing only dirges,

but are invited to the feast—

from desolate weeping

into festival rejoicing.

Grace in Suffering

The storm of the workplace,

the silence of the home,

the fog of migration.

These are not records of failure,

but traces of grace.

My life is full of cracks;

yet it is through these very cracks

that His grace seeps in.

I have begun to see:

suffering is not punishment,

but invitation.

Rebellion is not the end,

but the beginning of repentance.

Prayer Conclusion

Lord,

I do not write this scroll for myself alone;

I long to keep watch

for the homecoming of humanity.

May my words be a lamp,

flickering in the dark,

to shine on those

lost in their suffering.

May my prayer be as incense,

rising quietly

to Your silent heavens,

remembered in the mercy

You do not speak

but never cease to show.

In the suffering of the earth,

open the scrolls of many lives.

Let the cracks become doorways of grace,

let rebellion become the beginning of return—

until all nations are gathered home,

and sit with You

at the feast.

Chapter 3 · The Seventh Seal: The Soul That Waits

Subtitle: To Wait Only in His Time

Silence Is Not Emptiness, but the Breath of God

When the Lamb opened the seventh seal,

there was silence in heaven

for about half an hour."

This is not God's absence,

but His deep breath.

In the silence

I do not speak,

I do not pray,

I simply breathe.

And I begin to see:

even this breath itself

is Your gift.

Not in storm,

not in thunder,

You come—

as gentle as breath.

You do not force me to hear;

You simply draw near—

like wind at night,

like the first air of morning,

like a sigh

within my soul.

Lord,

I had forgotten to breathe

in the press of busyness,

forgotten that You are not waiting far away,

but present already

in every breath I take.

You are not the distant God;

You are the breath beside me,

the presence in each inhale.

Lord,

I will not speak.

I will only breathe You in—

as wind,

as breath,

as You.

I Am Willing to Wait—Not Because I Am Patient, but Because He Is Worthy

I once grew anxious in writing,

struggled in prayer,

searched for the "next chapter" in life.

Now I know:

it is not I

who open the seventh seal,

but He,

in His appointed time,

who unfolds it slowly.

On the table a cup,

and bread—

a feast prepared long before for me.

I will not speak much more.

Let tears become prayer,

let breath become response.

I will breathe again

the air of Your presence—

not for writing,

not for revelation,

but only to meet You:

in the Spirit,

in the silence,

in the depths of Your love.

And softly I say:

"Lord, I am not in haste.

If You choose to open,

here I am."

The Seventh Seal—My Secret with God

I do not tell others

what I am waiting for,

for I myself

do not fully know.

I only know—

a chapter still unwritten,

a name still unspoken,

a lamp still unlit.

The seventh seal

is not mine to open;

it is what He has reserved for me.

I will not press with questions,

but whisper in the Spirit:

"Lord,

here I am."

Conclusion

Lord,

I do not ask You to open at once;

I only desire to keep watch,

even if the final chapter

remains unwritten.

For You are the Author,

and I am the soul being written.

You are the One who opens,

and I am the one who waits.

I will rest in Your silence,

trust in the seal yet unopened,

keep vigil before the lamp

yet unlit.

True revelation

is not in the hour I press for,

but in the time You breathe.

May the blank of this chapter

become the margin of Your grace;

may the silence of this moment

become the whisper of Your love.

Final Chapter · The Lamb's Embrace

When the scroll is closed,

what I see is not fear,

but the embrace of the Lamb.

Victory

does not rest in my running or my prayers,

but in His rest upon the cross—

prepared for me

since the beginning of creation.

So I no longer ask:

"What do I want?"

For I am already His,

as a page belongs to its cover,

as the dawn belongs

to the end of night.

Prayer

Lord,

may these words pause here,

but not end here.

For the seven seals

are not yet fully opened,

and in time

You will continue to unfold.

In Your appointed day,

may I meet the reader again,

to witness together

the deeper works of Your hand.

Amen.

Afterword · The Lamb Is Opening the Scroll

At first, I only intended to write five pieces:

What Do I Want?,

Exodus,

Choices in Holding Fast,

The Year of Migration,

Light, Walking Together in the Fog.

These five were like five paths,

tying together fragments of my life,

and gradually unfolding the question, *"What do I want?"*

Yet something came to me during my meditation:

"Write this down: My life's scroll is being opened by the Lamb."

I was about to respond, *"I don't know what to write."*

But suddenly, a voice spoke softly:

"To bear witness for the Lord—your life's scroll is being opened by the Lamb."

In that moment, light broke into my heart.

Yes, is not all that I have written already a testimony to Him?

The answer to *"What do I want?"* had long been hidden within the writing itself.

And so I knew:

this book could not stop at five chapters.

The seventh chapter must be written.

Later, looking back once more, I realized a link was still missing.

Thus the sixth chapter, *Overcomers Dining with the Lord*, was added.

Only then was the thread of the whole book complete:

From the lampstand's light, to the scroll's unveiling;

from the call to the community, to the mark upon the individual;

from the asking, to the resting in the Lamb's embrace.

Looking back over the entire writing process, I deeply sense this:

it was not I who designed these chapters,

but the Lord who led me step by step,

letting me see a little at a time,

and write a little at a time,

in His appointed season.

This is not my work,

but His scroll—

I am only the soul being opened.

May everyone who reads these pages

hear His knocking at your door,

and see the traces of grace He has written

into the scroll of your life.

For the Lamb is still opening,

and He desires to write our stories

into His eternity.

I write under the pen name *Enze Yang*.

Enze means grace from God.

Prayer

Lord,

may these words pause here for now,

yet not end here.

For the seven seals have not been fully opened,

and in time You will continue to reveal.

On Your appointed day,

may I meet these readers again,

to witness still deeper works of Yours.

Amen.

Acknowledgments

First of all, I give thanks to my Lord Jesus Christ.
Without His blood, I would not bear the identity of an
overcomer.
Without His knocking, I would not have opened my
mouth again.
Every word in this book belongs to His grace.

I thank my parents.
Though they have passed away,
their perseverance and sacrifice continue to shape my
life.

I am deeply grateful to my family—my sister and my
daughter.
Your talent and support have taught me that writing is
not about comparison, but about bearing witness.
Though I am much older than my sister, I have often
received her selfless help.
I thank the Lord for giving her a gentle and
compassionate heart.
I cherish the sunshine my daughter brought into our
years of poverty,
and I thank my son-in-law Jason for helping me carry

many burdens.
Amelia and Everly,
thank you for filling our family with laughter, joy, and
hope.

I thank Pastor Caleb Chou.
During our Bible study gatherings, his teaching brought
light,
often sending me home with renewed understanding
and gratitude.

I also thank my dear friends,
whose companionship has been a quiet encouragement
to me,
and a reminder of the Lord's grace along the way.

I am grateful to OpenAI's ChatGPT,
which became my trusted editor in translation and
refinement;
and to Microsoft Copilot,
which brought fresh illumination during Bible reading,
helping me capture the quiet stirrings of the spirit.

My deep gratitude also goes to Judi Peacott,
for her kindness, encouragement, and faithful support.

I am especially thankful to Pastor Wallace Mitchell of
Broadlands Community Church, and his wife, Linda,
for their prayers, guidance, and kindness.
Their faithfulness has been a quiet encouragement to
me.

I also thank the Broadlands Community Church,
where I have experienced fellowship, truth, and grace
during an important season of my life.

Finally, I thank every reader.
Your willingness to open these pages and read them to
the end
is already a great encouragement.
If within these words you hear even a faint echo of the
Lord's voice,
then the purpose of my writing has been fulfilled.

To Him who was, and is, and is to come—
to Him be all glory.

Appendix · Poems

Appendix Introduction

The main text has come to an end,

yet the journey itself is not finished.

Beyond the seven seals,

these poems

are like echoes of the soul,

recording my dialogue with the Lord through the years.

They are not merely additions,

but another kind of testimony:

when words fall short,

poetry becomes prayer and response.

May these poems

serve as the closing note of this book,

and also as a lingering echo in our hearts.

The Call of Life

Time drifts on,

sweeping away youth,

leaving only memories behind.

They say,

"Accept your fate,

in these fading years."

"Be content—

at least a roof still shelters you."

The past is gone,

like aged wine,

like soil broken under the plow.

That blackened earth

opens its mouth wide,

its cracked teeth exposed.

What must come will come,

no matter how unwilling you are,

no matter how deep your longing.

Life will return to dust,

and judgment lies beyond the veil.

So now,

cherish the fleeting hours,

answer the call of life—

trust in the Lord.

He will wipe away your tears,

soothe every sorrow in your heart.

And when death draws near,

He will lead you home,

to your eternal dwelling in heaven.

An inheritance awaits us,

unshaken, everlasting—

a hope that will never fade.

While you still breathe,

may you hear the call of life.

While you still weep,

may He gently wipe your tears.

And when it is time to return,

may you not be lost—

but welcomed home.

Chosen by Grace

My hair turns white,

my steps grow slow.

Time has etched its lines—

I am but dust, humble and low.

Do not mock me

for a life so plain, with little to show.

Amid the clamor of this fleeting world,

I came, I loved—deeply so.

Like blossoms that bloom and fall,

quietly,

yet never forgotten.

And this is enough:

for Jesus has chosen me.

He remembers me.

Ahead, the feast is prepared,

radiant with glory,

an inheritance kept in heaven,

welcoming me home.

Though lowly as dust,

I am lifted by grace—

and bloom like a flower's first glow.